Backyards
and
Tiny Gardens

Backyards
and
Tiny Gardens

JUDITH BERRISFORD

Faber & Faber Limited
3 Queen Square · London

First published in 1976
by Faber and Faber Limited
3 Queen Square London WC1
Printed in Great Britain by
Western Printing Services Ltd, Bristol
All rights reserved

ISBN 0 571 11034 7 (hard bound edition)
ISBN 0 571 10837 7 (Faber Paperbacks)

Contents

Acknowledgements

I should like to express my thanks to Miss Yvonne Skargon for her skilful interpretation of my garden designs and for so kindly contributing two designs (1 and 12), one of her own small front garden and one which she planned for a friend. I feel I have been lucky in having an artist of such sensitivity and ability to illustrate my book.

I am grateful to my friend and editor, Eileen Brooksbank, for giving me the opportunity to express my own enthusiasm for gardening on so small a scale and I am also indebted to Ann Bonar for her helpful editorial advice.

PART ONE

CHAPTER ONE

Sows' ears

They used to say that the British were a shop-keeping nation – but I think it would be more true to call us a race of gardeners. There are few men – and even fewer women – in this country who have not at some time or another grown something; even if it was only a pan of mustard-and-cress or a pot of bulbs. Today, perhaps more than at any other time in our history, much of the leisure time of adult citizens is spent in gardening – whether in raising outsize greenhouse chrysanthemums, organically grown vegetables for the table, specimens for the show-bench, exotic foliage for cutting or South African violets and pot plants for the house.

Yet for every one person who can happily indulge his yearnings, either in his own garden or in an allotment plot, there are at least three more suffering from frustration because they do not have – or think they do not have – anywhere adequate to indulge their fancy. It is for these frustrated gardeners that this book is intended – for those people who want to grow something and to transform their own particular pig's ear – whether it be a backyard, basement strip, pocket-handkerchief front garden or scratching run for local cats at the rear – into something better; even though they may feel it can never really become a silk purse. It is, in fact, for men and women who want actually to garden, however limited their space. I would like to help them to bring a feeling of the country into their city street, housing development in minimum-gardened suburb, or pavement edging in a seaside town. I should like to give them the chance to find again their ancestral roots that, like those of eighty-five per cent of their fellow Britons, have their tips firmly in the soil of the countryside from which they sprang a few generations ago.

The type of plots I have in mind measure no more than $12\frac{1}{2}$ m (42 ft) long by $4\frac{1}{2}$ m (15 ft) wide – just over three times the size of the average small living room.* Some gardens may be even smaller; the very limitation of size is a challenge. In this book I want to help people to enjoy gardening in even the smallest plots so that they can make them into outdoor living areas in which it is a pleasure to sit. Above all, I would like to help people to grow something worthwhile in the space available, to enable them to have something pleasing to look at throughout the year, and to help them to create a satisfying garden. My aim is not to give instructions on how to build a classical temple in a London backyard; nor how to obtain romantic *trompe l'oeil* stage-set effects in such a situation; nor how to build a swimming pool. I am more concerned with helping real gardeners who like to call a spade a spade, and with encouraging them to use it to make a flowery patio or a green and growing garden from their backyard or basement patch. I would like to help the country-man or countrywoman inside so many urban dwellers whose basic need above all else is to grow plants, and to add a colourful dimension to outdoor living and a scenic backcloth to their home. Pocket gardens little more than 3½ m (12 ft) square can be made into oases of peace and beauty.

To do this, and in order to strain for the ultimate silk purse, one has to see each sow's ear clearly as it really is, without the rose-coloured spectacles of optimistic illusion. One has to face the dusty desert, complete with its ground-swamping bricks, its dank sour soil, its dustbins, coal-bunkers, central-heating oil tanks, and manhole covers. Exposure to neighbours and lack of privacy is accentuated, almost to the point at which it cannot be overcome, by the ubiquitous tower blocks. Even the mature apple tree or sycamore which brings a touch of greenery into some tiny gardens has its disadvantages, because in order to enable it to confer its bonus, its roots must starve everything else.

It is important to realize that each individual owner of a backyard or tiny garden has his own priorities. For one, it is a place in which to relax in the sun, to entertain friends, and to enjoy al fresco meals or drinks when the weather is warm and the sun shines. For another, it is somewhere to grow flowers and foliage to give cutting material for the house throughout the year. Some want to grow salads, herbs,

---

* Where appropriate, lengths over 3 ft have been converted into metres, rounding up or down to the nearest half metre. Lengths of 3 ft or under have been converted into centimetres, taking 30 cm as 1 ft.

strawberries and fruit, or to have the joy of picking their own scarlet
runners fresh from the plant. Some may decide to concentrate on
alpine gardening, others on roses and bulbs. Most people, however,
probably want a little of all these things – an aim which would not
be difficult to satisfy if all small plots had ideal soils and aspects. As
it is, in the hard, cold world of truth and without the aid of rose-
tinted spectacles, all requirements must be looked at in a practical
light and amended or modified in accordance with what is really
possible in the existing physical conditions.

When this is done fearlessly and the problems faced and overcome,
the smallest and most unpromising areas can give hours of rewarding
happiness. When we were first married my husband and I exchanged
the unrestricted acreage of a large country garden for a 4½ × 9 m
(15 × 30 ft) plot behind an urban semi-detached house. To make
matters worse the garden looked onto the uncompromising hardness
of commercial glasshouses. Yet with hard work and patience we were
able to transform that backyard into a semblance of a flower-filled
cottage garden.

With no room for more than essential paving, we crammed
each foot of soil with plants. Hollyhocks and delphiniums disguised
the wall of the next-door garage while a painted trellis blocked off
the glasshouses. We grew sweet peas up the trellis in summer
against a background of variegated ivy which helped to mask the
winter harshness of the glass. Window-boxes and hanging baskets
against the house and wash-house walls made vantage points for further
colour. Ivy and 'Double Golden Gleam' nasturtiums trailed down
from a trough, disguising the coal-barrel. Nasturtiums rioted also
around the base of the Grenadier apple tree.

Ferns, hostas, bergenias and Solomon's seal mingled with lilies-of-
the-valley, primulas, and lungwort to fringe the path of broken paving
that led from the kitchen to the wash-house door. Other shade-
tolerant subjects such as foxgloves, campanulas, astilbes, thalictrum,
day lilies and Japanese anemones filled the remaining space, because
the aspect of our tiny garden was north.

Only limited room was available for shrubs, but against the wall
that divided our backyard from the one next-door we sited *Hydrangea
paniculata* 'Grandiflora' for the glory of its greeny, creamy and pink-
tinged panicles. Behind, purple *Clematis* 'Jackmanii Superba'
intertwined with the golden 'Mermaid' rose.

In nooks and crannies between the plants we trowelled Spanish bluebells (*Endymion*) and narcissi with crocuses and muscari for spring. Schizostylis with their small gladioli-like spikes in pink and crimson were our chosen bulbous subjects for the end of the year. They mingled with the orange stigmas and violet-blue chalices of *Crocus speciosus*, the finest of the autumn-flowering crocuses.

The Grenadier apple-tree, a strawberry barrel and a clump of champagne rhubarb satisfied our craving to grow 'something to eat', along with a kitchen window-box of chives, parsley and radishes. Our other window-boxes appealed to the eye rather than the palate, with primroses and early pansies, followed by fuchsias and the luscious camellia-flowered tuberous begonias, the blooms of which are richer-coloured and longer lasting when grown away from the sun.

At that time we found this little garden entirely satisfying, though others might have different needs. Some may long for the greenery of growing grass, and even this might be incorporated in a tiny space, perhaps siting a square of green turf in contrast with paving textures, as others might site a pool. Or one could build a slightly raised circular bed – just one brick high – filling it with humus-containing loam and sowing grass seed there to make a miniature lawn. With different priorities, one might devote half one's space to grass, using it as a background for flowers and shrubs, letting in stepping stones of paving to take the wear, because often in the enclosed conditions of very small town gardens the soil grows sour and the turf becomes unduly sensitive. The smallness of the garden can make grass a rare commodity, the value of which can be enhanced by giving it an interesting emphasis or an unusual shape.

In a tiny garden space is so precious that every square foot counts. Every inch must be used to give its owners the maximum pleasure. If successfully planned, a small garden can have an impact and an intimacy that is seldom found in larger sites. Without even trying, it cannot help but be an extension of the house, vibrantly furnished with glowing colours, or restfully green and cool.

To cope with the lack of privacy from overlooking tall buildings, a pergola can be built over a paved terrace: over it can be grown a living canopy of scrambling or twining plants under which, screened, at least in part, from the overseeing gaze, one can eat or laze in summer.

Oil storage tanks and dustbins can be screened. Coal-bunkers can be topped with a decorative trough – at least for summer. A tub or concrete pot filled with flowers will adequately disguise an inspection cover.

Even the smallest garden, if it is to be satisfying, needs to be worked out on paper. Plan in pencil, so that you can use an india-rubber, until you have a design that is practical and that satisfies you. Or you can cut out shapes of different coloured papers to scale, representing flower beds, seats, a table, grass or pool, moving them about on the basic sheet that represents your site until you have arranged them to make the most of the available space.

Bear in mind, too, the question of aspect. A site that faces north may be suitable for sitting out in only at its furthest end. It should be planted with shade-loving subjects. Its walls may be painted white or cream to reflect the light. On the other hand, in a sunny plot you may want to create shade and an illusion of coolness. It is not for nothing that the gardens of the Mediterranean countries have a summer plan based on greenery and the splash of water. But tiny gardens, such as we are thinking of, must be capable, particularly in this climate, of offering enjoyment in all types of weather. They should be planned to make attractive and effective backgrounds for the indoor living space of the house at all seasons and, if possible, to yield material for arrangement indoors during every month of the year.

CHAPTER TWO

Problems, practicalities and paving

Most backyards, to start with at any rate, have only a few narrow beds for flowers (some have none at all until spaces are cleared). The rest of the soil might be covered by yard bricks, paving stones or concrete slabs. Even with these coverings raised and stacked, what soil there is – deprived of air and light as it has been – will be sour and dank.

The first and main problem of the tiny garden, once the design has been decided upon and the growing areas allotted, is to revivify the soil. The ideal solution to the problem of sick, sour soil would, of course, be to remove it to a depth of two spits and replace it with good loam. But in some cases this can be extremely difficult to carry out, perhaps because the only access to the garden is through the living space of the house. Some are more fortunate in that their backyards or pocket gardens are serviced by an alleyway with a gate through which to barrow the soil. Even then, the old worn-out soil has to be disposed of. Probably the simplest way of accomplishing this is to obtain the services of a trustworthy builder or garden construction firm who will remove the old soil, provide good topsoil, and spread it over the required areas. This, today, can be costly, so the majority will want to settle for something less drastic.

A dressing of hydrated lime at the rate of 0·46 kg per sq m (1 lb per sq yd) will do much to counteract the sourness of the soil, but it should not be used where azaleas or heathers are to be grown. Instead, gypsum can be used, as it will do the same job without altering the alkalinity of the soil. It is not enough, in any case, just to combat soil sickness. Fertility must also be restored by adding manure, either organic in the form of horse or cow manure or rotted garden compost, or artificial, in which case it is safest to use a complete concentrated fertilizer of a proprietary sort. Otherwise it is only too easy to upset the balance of the soil or to mix incompatible materials together. For instance, nitro-chalk and sulphate of ammonia should not be mixed with basic slag, chalk or any substance containing lime, while lime should not be mixed with nitrogenous fertilizers, animal manures or soot before being dug into the soil. A period of several weeks at least should elapse after the limy substance has been applied.

It is important correctly to assess the needs of the soil, and to this end it is worth investing a few pounds on one of the better soil-testing kits, such as that marketed by Sudbury Technical Products of 58 Charlton Road, London SE3 8TT, which not only helps to determine whether the soil is acid or alkaline but also points out the deficiencies of any vital elements and recommends appropriate treatment.

To renovate or renew all the soil in the garden, however small, could be a mammoth task, but it is not too difficult to renew the top 15 cm (6 in), removing the existing top layer from the beds and perhaps using it as a foundation for raised beds elsewhere to vary the level and to bring plants nearer the light. Border carnations, dianthus, many of the pleasant silver-leaved plants and some alpines also benefit from the sharper drainage conferred by the raising of the level. Surplus yard bricks can be used to build up low retaining walls, thus making a virtue of necessity and adding considerably to the character and charm of the garden. If one decides to do this, it is then only necessary to bring in a smaller quantity of soil for the top layer. One might even simply surround all the proposed beds with 15 cm (6 in) walls and top them up with good soil to the new level.

If this is decided upon it is important first to break up the existing soil, digging in a quantity of peat, bonemeal and hoof and horn. Further improvement may be effected over the seasons by the use of a compost bin in which garden and household waste may be stacked, treated with a reliable accelerator such as Garotta or Comprot, and rotted down to a dark brown, sweet-smelling compost of crumbly consistency with which to mulch the garden. The Compo-Quick Company of Deerhurst, Walton, Glos., offer enclosed bins, made in dark green, high-density, expanded polystyrene which are ideal for compost-making in the tiny garden. Rotocrop Ltd of 848 Brighton Road, Purley, Surrey also offer an 'Accelerator' compost bin together with a useful booklet on compost-making. By using these containers and following the directions on the accelerator packet one can be assured of satisfactorily made compost. Into the bin all fallen leaves, grass clippings, soft stems and cut-down herbaceous material may be mixed, along with chopped-up banana skins, orange and grapefruit halves, apple peel, tea leaves, cabbage stalks, pea shucks and similar kitchen waste.

Seaweed is a great source of natural organic fertilizer. For centuries the farmers and gardeners of Cornwall, Wales, the Scilly Isles, the Hebrides and the Channel Islands have used it to increase the fertility of the ground, and I am glad to say that seaweed is now available to inland gardeners in crushed dried form. It is imported from Brittany by Rye Shipping Ltd, Rye, Sussex, from whom it can be bought in quantities ranging from 10 kg (22 lb) upwards. A 10-kg (22-lb) bag will provide enough basic treatment for $7\frac{1}{2}$ sq m (80 sq ft) of soil. Maere Seaweed is entirely free of any chemical additives. Another firm, Maxicrop Ltd, supply a liquid seaweed manure, which can be obtained from most ironmongers and garden supply shops.

Composted stable manure can also be bought, and advertisements for Cuttings Compost and Elliott's Stable Manure will be seen in the gardening pages of many newspapers and in the specialist press.

All these sources of humus are particularly valuable to the owner of a tiny garden, improving the soil and at the same time providing nutriment in a clean, smell-free and easy-to-handle form. Car owners may like to keep a sack or two in the boot of the car for use when visiting the country or the sea. Dead leaves, leaf-mould, cut bracken and seaweed may then be collected, either to be added to the compost or to be used as a mulch around shrubs, roses or climbers.

Of course, in the tiniest gardens, soil-less composts based on peat, such as Levington Potting or Kerimure, may be used, although they would prove too expensive to be practical on a larger scale. For troughs, containers, shallow raised beds or brick-contained boxes the soil-based John Innes potting compost No. 3 might also be used.

Some backyards and tiny garden patches may consist of clay soil which, untreated, is the gardener's nightmare, although properly dealt with it can be among the most fertile of growing mediums. Various proprietary forms of treatment exist, among the best of which are the gypsum-based Aerosoil, the seaweed-based Break-through and the now well-tried Acta-Bacta, which my husband and I have found most effective.

Many tiny gardens are dark, and in such cases the walls should be painted or distempered white or cream to trap and intensify all the available light. This fulfils an aesthetic purpose, too, forming a wonderful background for wall pots of colourful pelargoniums, spring bulbs or variegated ivy.

In some towns, air pollution is still a problem, although Clean Air Acts have done much to make the life of city gardeners easier. Sometimes minimal pollution can be helpful in keeping down black spot and other fungal disorders, but in some districts it is still possible to grow only the toughest of the evergreens. In such areas it is best to concentrate on deciduous plants which renew their foliage each spring rather than on evergreens, which tend to become defoliated and maimed by retaining their leaves through the winter, when smoke, smog, hail and sleet accentuate the damage of atmospheric pollution and chemical fall-out. In this case one has to rely on decorative walls and screening to supply the framework of the garden which might otherwise have been provided, in part at any rate, by evergreens.

In clean air districts, the garden owner must hesitate before annoying his neighbours by using an incinerator, and this can produce problems at pruning time. The best solution, I think, is to chop up woody stems which are difficult to compost and add them to the domestic refuse in the dustbin. By keeping a watchful eye on growth throughout the year, it is usually possible to cut things back a little week by week, and so avoid a major disposal problem.

Most people will want somewhere to sit out of doors so that they can take advantage of days that are pleasantly warm and sunny. In the sheltered conditions of a town garden, this probably means that they will be able to enjoy some stolen hours of sunshine in early spring as well as summer. For this purpose a part of the garden should be paved. Where yard bricks exist, enough may be left down to form a sitting area. True, blue-black yard bricks are not among the most attractive of paving materials, but if the sitting area is furnished with some of the lightweight, white patio furniture now available, and with tubs or barrels painted white, they can make a pleasant background, particularly if some of the surplus bricks, lifted to make more growing space elsewhere in the yard, are used to form a path in herring-bone or other formal pattern so as to add motif to the whole.

All tiny gardens, however, have not been backyards, and often their owners will have to start their paving from scratch. This can be difficult in plots with restricted access, and in such places random or broken 'crazy' paving may have to be used, so that the materials can be carried in piece by piece. In Wales I have seen small slabs of slate from the mountains, and flattish stones from the local beach, set in cement and used to form decorative and original paving effects.

A method of do-it-yourself paving which we have found useful came from a tip picked up from one of the correspondents to the Royal Horticultural Society's Journal. It consists of laying random paving on top of heavy black polythene spread over well-weeded earth, brushing a dry mortar of cement and sand (2 parts dry sand to 1 of cement by bulk) thickly over the paving, and allowing the rain to wash it in. This method can be improved upon by spreading builder's or sea sand over the area to be paved and tamping it flat with a board before putting down the polythene. In some circumstances, however, drainage can present a problem when the polythene method is used, and so the paving should always be slanted slightly towards a grid. A great advantage is that the work can be done in sections as the stone or slate comes to hand, completing a few yards' stretch at a time. With plants encouraged to spill over and soften the edges a very pleasant effect can be achieved.

A more conventional method of paving is first to clean the ground as before, making sure that there are no horse-tail, couch grass or ground elder roots remaining to throw up shoots and cause trouble, then to put down a 7·5-cm (3-in) layer of ash, cinders or stone to form a drainage stratum as well as to provide a firm bed for the paving. Each stone should then be bedded in cement, also filling up the joins between the stones. Here and there, pockets should be made in the drainage and the joins and the cement kept clear. These can later be filled with good soil or compost and planted with such small hummocky subjects as thyme, thrift, alpine phlox or dwarf campanulas, *Sisyrinchium bermudianum* (the blue-eyed grass) or sedums. Flowering in succession throughout the season, they will add considerably to the charm. Pocket plants of this type will help the paving to drain also by absorbing surface water.

Paving laid straight onto soft ground should always have the ground rammed hard beforehand. Where plenty of wear is expected, it may also pay to lay down a 5-cm (2-in) bed of concrete before paving is attempted. This may require professional help. Wherever paving is laid near the house, care must be taken to prevent water draining into the foundations: that is why it is so important to slope the stones towards drainage grids. The correct fall to be allowed is 2·5 cm (1 in) in 1½ m (5 ft). Where no drainage system exists, it helps if the paving is sloped towards a little pool or even a water-greedy plant such as a dwarf willow or dwarf pampas grass or a coarse-rooted herbaceous subject such as *Ligularia* 'Desdemona' with its large purple-lined leaves and spectacular orange daisies.

Specially suited to tiny gardens are the smaller paving materials such as bricks, tiles, granite setts and cobblestones. If bricks are chosen they should be hard-burnt or engineering bricks, which will not disintegrate in frost. Bricks should be laid flat with the larger face showing, or on edge if a herringbone or square pattern is wanted.

Whichever paving is chosen, it may be varied with squares of cement in which interestingly shaped or well-coloured pebbles are set. This change of texture adds emphasis to the area. Another idea is to make a panel 'bed' of this type on which to set tubs or cement 'planters'. Change of texture deliberately used can help greatly in small gardens where paving predominates, seeming to add space and giving a more sophisticated, planned appearance.

Possible sources of supply for paving materials are the engineering and surveying departments of the local authorities, building and demolition firms, and garden centres. If you live near a quarry or a brick or tile works, you may be able to negotiate successfully for surplus material or 'seconds'. Redland Precast Ltd, Barrow-upon-Soar, Loughborough, Leics., supply interesting prefabricated paving materials, including some hexagonal paving slabs which are useful for making a long narrow yard look wider than it really is.

In damp weather some types of paving, especially brick or tile, are apt to become slippery with moss. To defeat this, Murphy's Super Moss Killer (obtainable from ironmongers and garden supply shops) can be used. The directions state that a quantity of 2 fl oz dissolved in 2 gal of water is enough to treat 8 sq yd (roughly, 57 ml in 9 l water for 8 sq m, in metric measurement). The treatment may have to be repeated if moss starts to grow again.

The smaller the garden, the greater in proportion should be the provision for planting space, not only at ground level but in the form of wall pots, troughs, hanging baskets, window-boxes, tower pots or strawberry planters, even an old horse manger, - all can be used. Screens – to hide oil tanks, compost bin or refuse bins – offer homes for scrambling plants. Even the top of the garden wall can have its plant boxes.

At ground level, the beds must be arranged with a sense of design in order to improve the aspect of the tiny garden as a whole. To increase the effect of space it may pay to use an asymmetrical design; for instance, the garden will look larger with a wide bed on only one of the boundaries. The grass or paving on the other side may then be taken almost to the base of the wall, leaving just a narrow strip suitable for planting climbers and wall shrubs.

In Part Two of the book will be found a section consisting of plans, explaining and suggesting various design principles that can be incorporated in order to make the most of the various types of small garden. If your own garden is smaller than some of those described, you will find it relatively simple to adapt the plans to suit the space available.

CHAPTER THREE

Priorities and preferences

In the tiny garden every bit of ground must be made to count, but however keen one may be on growing plants most of us still want room to relax – even if it is only a few feet of paving on which to put our chairs. Some town gardens, surrounded as they often are by high walls, have their own built-in privacy. Others, due to the present prevalence of high-rise flats and offices, may be so overlooked as to render sitting out almost distasteful. In such cases, the provision of some kind of overhead screening for the sitting area is an absolute priority.

Screenage of this type can be most effectively built in the form of a pergola, with cross-pieces overhead to carry climbing plants, or as an open-sided arbour – with corner posts supporting side trellis work and with a roof either of asbestos sheeting or of ridged perspex to confer a degree of privacy.

If the arbour or pergola is built against the garden wall, bricks may be removed and the cross-beams set in for greater strength and permanency. These and the corner support posts should be of hardwood to ensure durability. Teak or red cedar may be used in their natural state and oiled to resist the weather. Oak, and various imported timbers, will last better and look more attractive if painted white, or they can be treated with one of the proprietary wood preservers available.

The framework into which any trellis laths are fitted should also be of hardwood. Where they are to support a solid roof or overhead cross-beams which may carry a heavy weight of creeper growth, the corner posts and all supports should be of timber 15 cm (6 in) square. The top bearers should be 20 × 15 cm (8 × 6 in) and cross-members 20 × 5 cm (8 × 2 in). Bases of all support beams which are set into the ground should be proofed against decay and, if possible, set into concrete for additional strength.

The sides of such an arbour could be filled in with trellis sections to make it easier for climbing plants such as honeysuckle or vines to find a hold and to facilitate the tying in of clematis or roses. Square trellis, to my mind, always looks better than diamond mesh, and, if custom-made, should be in 15- or 20-cm (6- or 8-in) squares. Trellis of this type, painted white, may be used to disguise ugly walls or, by affording a change of texture, can add variety and the illusion of greater space to a very small garden. More practically, on account of the space between the trellis and the wall, dead leaves are less likely to collect to harbour slugs, snails and other pests.

The walls of tiny gardens offer important surfaces up which to grow suitable shrubs and climbers, thus giving another dimension. But not everyone wants to go to the expense or trouble of covering walls with trellis. On the other hand, it is useful to have something to which plants can be tied. A method we have found satisfactory is to peg panels of Netlon, or other plastic mesh, to the wall. The plants can then be trained to these. This necessitates less knocking about of the wall than the fixing of ties every few feet, as used to be done in old gardens.

Access to all parts of the garden is just as important in a small area as in a large – perhaps even more so since one of the joys of a tiny garden, especially in an urban area, is that one can slip out quickly to pick herbs or flowers, or just to enjoy the air and the plants, in any dry spell. One should therefore ensure that all corners are served by a path. The lawn, too, even if it is little more than the decorative rug of greenery which may be all the tiny available space can accommodate, should have stepping stones, enabling one to cross it dry-shod in all weathers and to avoid excessive wear to the turf.

In such a limited space, a decision must be reached as to the right balance between shrubs and perennials on the one hand and annuals or biennials on the other. The tiny garden that eschews all bedding plants can sometimes be a disappointment in the early years when cherished shrubs flower sparsely; but to fill all the beds with similar, long-blooming, bedding subjects such as the too often seen white alyssum, blue lobelia and scarlet salvias would be anathema to me. It is my belief that seasonal bedding should be confined to two or three focal areas – perhaps entirely in, or supplemented by, window-boxes or tubs of concentrated bloom. One should forget also the more conventional schemes and strive for more subtle effects, such as that contained in a scheme I saw recently where sweetly scented purple heliotrope, backed by small bushes of pink and purple fuchsia, were overhung by soft pink bells suspended from the angel's fishing rods of the wand flower – *Dierama pulcherrimum*.

Such bedding schemes can be expensive when one has no facilities for raising one's own plants, but against the fairly high cost should be set the very real advantage of giving the garden a guaranteed-successful, almost instant fillip. Besides, the cost, even of luxury bedding plants, is very low when compared with the cost of cigarettes, drinks, cosmetics, or even the new curtains, cushions or carpets in which one may invest with barely a second thought.

All life styles are based on the determination of personal priorities, and this is particularly true when considering the kind of garden one wants to provide as a background to, and an extension of one's home. For my husband and me it is important to have somewhere to grow the kind of plants we enjoy, including those which will provide us with material it is a pleasure to arrange for the house through all the months of the year; and, as well, to have an outdoor living space in which to relax.

However limited my space, I would always try to find room against a wall or fence for one of the *Camellia × williamsii* hybrids, of which one of the best is the well-known 'Donation', with its glowing, semi-double blossoms of warm pink. Camellias do not do well in alkaline soils, but in the tiny garden where the soil is not right for them it is a comparatively simple matter to grow a specimen in a tub (see Chapter Fifteen).

Another worthwhile wall shrub is an evergreen ceanothus with its neat, dark leaves and blue thimble-shaped heads of flowers. The hybrid 'Burkwoodii' is one of the best and longest blooming. Espalier-trained on a wall, in conjunction with the single, yellow rose 'Mermaid', it is delightful, and both will go on flowering from June almost all through the summer.

Berrying subjects are often sited against walls. Some of these, especially the early orange-fruited *Pyracantha* 'Lalandei', can be disappointing as the birds often take the berries almost as soon as they ripen. Feathered marauders do not seem so tempted by the yellow-berried forms. *Pyracantha* 'Buttercup' and the earlier 'Shawnee' are worth planting (both are obtainable from Hillier's of Winchester). Up them may be trained reliable clematis, such as the purple 'Jackmanii Superba' or the striped 'Nelly Moser', which will benefit from having the rigid framework of the firethorn up which to scramble. The early clematis flowers will then contrast with, or complement, the foamy froth of white pyracantha blossom, while the later blooms and berries will secure a continuity of interest.

Ivies are wall-covering plants which will cling without being tied in or supported. One of the best, and one which is hardy throughout the south and west, is the beautiful *Hedera canariensis* 'Variegata', an ivy from the Canary Islands with large leaves in two shades of green, variegated with cream, and tinged, in cold weather, with pink.

These are some of the permanent plantings for which I would always try to make space, together with one or two hydrangeas, fuchsias, and the male form of the tall-growing wall shrub *Garrya elliptica*, the grey-green, fringed catkins of which may reach up to 45 cm (18 in) in length and are so valuable for winter cutting.

Some may prefer to turn their backyard or pocket-sized plot into a rose garden, with hybrid teas or floribundas dominating the formal planting. Here, tiny bulbs might be interset to add colour in spring when the hard-pruned bushes are bare. Rock plants such as dianthus, *Campanula cochlearifolia* and *C. carpatica*, sedums, thrift and thymes might be used to soften the edges of the beds and to spill onto the paving. Dwarf lavender, backed by the dwarf purple *Berberis thunbergii atropurpurea*, might be used to edge the sitting out area, where tubs of wallflowers, tulips and Brompton stocks for spring could add colourful emphasis, giving place in summer to softly toned, pleasantly fragrant petunias, pink and white pelargoniums, and the jewel tones of asters or dwarf dahlias in harvest festival colours.

Herbaceous plants such as foxgloves, delphiniums, lupins and *Campanula persicifolia*, hardy geraniums such as the blue *G. grandiflorum* and the pink *G. endressii*, the lime-green *Alchemilla mollis*, hostas and bergenias often all do extremely well in the sheltered conditions of tiny walled-in gardens. They can be interspersed with lilies and other summer bulbs such as dwarf gladioli and the tall creamy spires of the Cape hyacinth – *Galtonia candicans* – and perhaps flanked by a small shrub such as *Hebe elliptica* or a potentilla. More statuesque plants such as the yuccas with their ivory spikes, the dwarf bamboo *Arundinara nitida*, rheums, and *Senecio cineraria* with its white kid leaves, can also be used to give increased depth to the tiny garden.

Iris pallida 'Variegata' and the smaller spurges may also have a place. To make the most of them, one might copy an idea from New Zealand and make a pebble bed. First the soil is prepared by digging in a good quantity of moist peat, then good loam and gravel is added, or John Innes potting compost No. 3. A sheet of heavy black polythene is spread over the surface, to prevent the encroachment of weeds. Crosses are cut in the polythene at each planting site and the edges are turned back so that planting may be carried out through the resultant holes. When all the plants are in place, shingle, pebbles or shale is added, to cover the polythene completely. The result is a trouble-free and most attractive bed in the Japanese style.

Hellebores could be added for winter interest. The pebbles and polythene would completely prevent any splashing or staining of the cups of the Christmas rose – *Helleborus niger* – while the Corsican hellebore – *H. lividus* 'Corsicus' – and the native *H. foetidus* with their green chalices and decorative leaves would look most effective. Some of the decorative grasses might also be used, especially the dwarf blue *Festuca glauca*, *Millium effusum* 'Aureum' – Bowles' golden grass – and *Miscanthus sinensis* 'Zebrinus', the striped zebra grass. Evergreen azaleas and the dwarf Japanese maples also look good in such a setting. One can, in fact, build up a bed that is aesthetically pleasing, mainly on the appeal of foliage and habit. Flowers there will be, of course, but, while no doubt appreciated, their appearance will be almost incidental.

These pebble beds, by their very nature, are formal in character. But then most tiny gardens have to be formal. Their lack of space necessitates orderliness. The most informality that can be allowed within their confines is that type of free-flowering luxuriance within a strictly rigid framework that characterizes the great gardens of Sissinghurst and Hidcote, and that has earned for this type of particularly English gardening the name of 'Paradise Gardening'. It is noteworthy that both these famous gardens, though covering many acres, consist in their better-known and more typical aspects of a series of small garden 'rooms' or sections – some no bigger than the type of plot considered in this book.

CHAPTER FOUR

Existing deserts

So far, we have tended to consider the planning of new gardens, or the reconstruction of the old, from 'scratch', as it were. Everyone, however, may not want to go to the expense and trouble of entirely redesigning their backyards or pocket plots. What, may they ask, can they do with an existing dusty desert, perhaps with a small, threadbare lawn, a few straggly roses and a mature tree, the roots of which rob everything within near reach?

In these days of hormone weedkillers it is comparatively easy to eradicate lawn weeds, but in the shut-up, airless confines of a tiny town garden, weeds are unlikely to be the major problem. Rather, it will be the sparseness of grass and the presence of moss encouraged by a dankness and poverty of soil, that will be causing the trouble.

It would be wise to give the lawn a feed of 14 g ($\frac{1}{2}$ oz) sulphate of ammonia to the sq m (sq yd), at least a fortnight before the application of the selective hormone. Nowadays, weedkillers are available to deal with a wide variety of invaders. Choice is best based on the type of weeds predominating in your patch. For initial treatment, I think that liquid weedkillers are best, although in subsequent years you may decide that it will be sufficient to use one of the dry compounds such as that produced by Fisons, combining the purposes of selective weed-killing with a lawn food.

Be sure to choose a still, warm day, when the soil is moist, for the treatment. Then mix the preparation in an old watering can, according to the instructions. If possible, it is wisest to keep a watering can especially for the job, marking it clearly with red paint or tying a red ribbon round the handle so that it is used for no other purpose. To water seedlings or bedding plants from a can that still contains the slightest trace of hormone weedkiller can be disastrous, as hormone weedkillers act by over-stimulating the growth of broad-leaved plants.

It is usually necessary to make two applications of the weedkiller at the intervals stated on the bottle. Keep exactly to the instructions and do not be tempted to give an extra strong dose or you may damage the grass without really killing the weeds. Too strong a solution withers the leaves before they have properly absorbed the weedkiller, and the plant springs to life refreshed.

Be careful not to let the solution splash or drift onto any nearby plants. I once lost a rose bush through this and am now particularly careful to do the job on a completely still day. Mowings from the treated lawn are unsafe to use as a mulch for at least six weeks following the last treatment; though they can be put on the compost heap provided it is not used until rotted thoroughly to a dark brown crumbly mass.

Hormone weed-killing treatment for the lawn is best carried out in April or May. This is the time when the weeds will be growing most vigorously, and so will be most damaged. In any case the whole lawn will benefit from a feed with a good lawn fertilizer put on beforehand.

In the type of garden we are considering, lawn areas will be small, so it will pay to use the best possible seed mixture. Carters supply lawn mixtures to suit any aspect, whether sunny or in shade and to suit varying degrees of wear. Thomson and Morgan Ltd of London Road, Ipswich, Suffolk, market a fine new mixture called 'Emerald Isle'. This has the advantage that it can be sown at any time from April to October, provided watering is carried out if the weather is dry. It establishes itself very quickly. Even more important, it spreads quickly into a dense, deep green sward that does not need too frequent cutting. This goes a long way towards avoiding the bare, hard-packed look which so often characterizes backyard lawns. This is a useful seed to take care of any bare patches, and the whole lawn may be improved by scattering it lightly over the grass in early October, adding a top-dressing of leaf-mould or moist granulated peat and brushing it well in.

Existing pocket 'deserts' and backyard 'sows' ears' often contain sooty, overgrown thickets of forsythia, ribes and mock orange, with one or two densely suckering lilacs that hardly justify the name of 'shrubs'. With these one must be drastic. If the lilacs bear good flowers, thin out or split up the clumps in late autumn, removing alternate shoots from the base. If they are so tall that most of the blossom is borne out of reach, then cut them back. Cutting back from the top will mean the sacrifice of a season's bloom, as it is done in early spring, but the garden will benefit in later years. Normally however, all pruning of lilacs should be done from the base. Otherwise, all that is necessary is the removal of faded flower heads, taking care not to damage the basal buds from which the following year's flowers will spring.

The same principle should be followed with the other shrubs, thinning shoots out from the spring-flowering types in autumn and cutting back summer subjects, such as buddleias, in March. Tangled clematis should be pruned in late February, cutting the large-flowered late summer-flowering hybrids back to within about 1 m (3 or 4 ft) of the main stems. The early summer-flowering kinds need not be treated so drastically, simply thinning and cutting back shoot tips to still dormant buds.

Straggly, poor-foliaged, rose bushes should be cut back hard in March, pruning to an outward-facing bud and using a slanting cut to take any moisture away from the axil of the bud. This principle is a sound one to follow, whatever the subject of the pruning.

Beware of cutting back flowering shrubs to square or rounded shapes as one might prune honeysuckle or privet. The arching wands of weigela or philadelphus and the burgeoning shoots of forsythia and berberis have a beauty that is entirely lost if they are clipped to hard unnatural shapes. Instead, cut out all unwanted or tangled wood from the base, remembering never to cut away more than a third of the growth at a time.

An exception to the rule of basal pruning is chaenomeles, which used to be known as cydonia or sometimes familiarly but incorrectly as 'japonica'. This will flower more freely if cut back to short, spurred side shoots in July or early August, as one does with trained apples or pears. The frilly-flowered, bright pink *Prunus triloba* also benefits from this type of treatment.

To renovate an old flower border, it is wisest to wait until the autumn. Then one can lift and divide all the old clumps of perennials, retaining the outer shoots and throwing away the worn-out centres. Only peonies, lilies, hellebores, eremurus and other exceptionally long-lived or touchy subjects should remain undisturbed. When the border is clear (and its occupants safely laid on sacking so that the soil on their roots does not muddy the lawn or paths and so tread into the house) one can renovate the soil by forking in a good ration of rotted manure or garden compost, together with a dressing of bonemeal at about 50 g (2 oz) per sq m (sq yd).

Clumps of bulbs will also benefit from being divided. Daffodils, however, do not enjoy manure, preferring a dressing of leaf-mould. If this is not available a small quantity of moist peat, dug into the ground before replanting, will help to improve the nature of the soil.

Adding carpeting rock plants as 'edgers' to trail over the bricks, or to soften the path, will often improve the effect. When refurbishing an old garden, one should try to add plants with an extended season of interest or of particular merit such as *Mahonia japonica*, which adds fragrant winter blossom to its handsome evergreen leaves. Existing shrubs may often be brightened by the addition of a clematis, planted outside the root area in a pocket of good soil and given a cylinder of Netlon or other plastic netting to protect the stem and lead it into the outer branches.

Poor condition of the soil must, I am afraid, be taken for granted in most old town gardens. Wherever possible the soil should be treated by digging in peat, compost or manure, or at least given a top-dressing of good soil. Existing shrubs and rose bushes may be helped by mulching with rooted compost or manure or even by pricking in bonemeal, Toprose or a similar fertilizer in spring and autumn. Annual top-dressing should be a matter of routine.

A mature tree is really a priceless asset, conferring character and natural shade. The detrimental effect of the roots may to some extent be offset, and the decorative aspect of the feature increased, by building a raised bed 45 cm (18 in) or so in height over the immediate root area and walling it with bricks. Filled with good soil, such a bed offers a home for primroses, pansies, petunias, semperflorens begonias, small fuchsias or other attractive plants.

All in all, the planning of a tiny garden is a matter of personal preferences, depending on the amount of time and – to some extent – money one is prepared to expend. To be successful, it must be a reflection, to a great extent, of one's own particular tastes and needs.

CHAPTER FIVE

Cutting the cost and raising your stock

As inflation spirals higher year by year, the factor of cost, even in the tiny garden, cannot be ignored. As I said previously, the amount of money one can put into one's garden is a matter of personal priorities. Few of us these days can afford to spend as much as we would like on our hobbies. The cost of new garden furniture may have to be weighed against the cost of new covers for the sitting room chairs. One person may decide that the outdoor living area should have priority, another may choose to spend the money on beautifying the house. Career women may even be faced with the difficult choice of whether to buy a load of topsoil for the garden or choose a new winter coat. The decision will depend on the degree of importance the garden plays in the life style of each individual.

Within the garden itself, one again has to set the cost against the benefit the proposed expenditure may confer. Busy people will rate high the saving of time and the almost guaranteed satisfaction gained by buying ready-grown plants for 'instant' gardening, as against the effort, time-consumption and possible frustration incurred by attempting to raise one's own plants from cuttings or seed when one has neither the space nor the proper facilities to do so.

In the challenging conditions of many draughty and light-starved town gardens, the raising of plants from seed and cuttings may be difficult. It is better in such cases to buy established plants, whether they be petunias or antirrhinums for the summer bedding or shrubs for permanent positions. Given minimum facilities, however, such as a tiny greenhouse, a glass-roofed sun porch or a mini-propagator, the raising of seedlings and cuttings becomes a viable proposition.

One of the simplest small propagators is the Humex Pottagator, consisting of an electrically heated base with a tray for seeds or cuttings and a clear, lightweight plastic cover to conserve moisture and obtain humidity. Another small propagator is marketed by Camplex, who also specialize in supplying self-watering pots and troughs. Their propagator consists of a deep plastic trough in which an electric heating cable is embedded in a layer of sand. An adjustable rod thermostat controls the temperature and the trough is covered with a 25-cm (10-in) high polythene dome, giving adequate headroom for young plants and cuttings. Measuring about 60 × 75 cm (2 × 2½ ft), it is big enough to enable one to raise several batches of seeds and cuttings at a time.

When considering investing in one of these, it is necessary to consider not only the initial seed-raising or striking of cuttings but the provision of an 'after-care' unit in the shape of a frame, sun porch or greenhouse for hardening off and growing on. A simple frame may be made from a wooden box, with the bottom knocked out, which is cut down on one side so as to slant towards the sun. Such a box should stand on a bed of ashes. Seed-trays or pots of young plants may then be set on the ashes. A sheet of glass or clear plastic to enclose it completes the frame, and in order to harden off the plants one has merely to raise the glass, increasing the gap by a few inches each day until it can be removed altogether during the hours of daylight. A mat or sacking and one or two thicknesses of newspaper should be kept in readiness to place over the glass on frosty nights.

If there is no propagator, however, but only a sunny window sill, or even an unheated sun porch or greenhouse, one is limited as to what one can do towards raising one's own plants. In such conditions, it should be possible at least to strike and over-winter cuttings of the more expensive bedding subjects such as pelargoniums, heliotrope and fuchsias. One could grow on dahlias and large-flowered begonias from tubers, saving these from year to year, and one might even root simple shrubs such as hydrangeas or lavender from cuttings.

Tuberous begonias can be bought as dry corms in March and started off singly in 12-cm (5-in) pots which can later be sunk into window-boxes or other containers and packed with peat. Alternatively, if it is intended to plant the begonias out into garden beds, they can be raised three to a 17-cm (7-in) pot in seed-trays. Levington compost or John Innes potting compost No. 2 are ideal, or, if they are later to be transferred to the garden, one can start off the tubers in moist peat only. As with hardy cyclamen, it is sometimes a puzzle to tell which side of the begonia tuber is the top. In fact, the upper side is usually hollow or flat and has an area where the old stem grew which is clear of wispy roots. This should be kept uppermost.

Crock the pots or trays and half fill with compost. Sit the tubers on the compost and pack in more compost until the tuber is first covered. Then stand the pots on a light window sill or put them in the sun porch or cold frame. The compost should be kept moist, but care should be taken not to over-water the pots until growth starts, otherwise the tubers may rot. Once the shoots appear, they should be shaded from strong sunshine or the leaves may be scorched. Gradually harden them off and then put them into their positions for the summer once frost danger is past.

Dahlias may be over-wintered safely if they are lifted from the ground after the first frost. The blackened leaves and stems should be cut down, leaving only about 5 cm (2 in) of stem, to which you can attach a label indicating variety and colour. They may then be packed into a box of dry peat. In March they should be given a little water to start them into growth and transferred to the cold frame as soon as the shoots appear. Cover well during frosty weather and do not transfer to the garden until all frosts are past.

Pelargoniums, gazanias, gerberas, arctotis and similar expensive bedding subjects, as well as penstemons and heliotrope, may also be over-wintered as growing plants if they are cut down and lifted in late autumn, set in pots of well-drained compost, taken into an unheated room, and watered lightly to keep them just growing through the winter. Fuchsias will also survive if given similar treatment, but they do not need to be cut down; they can be pruned back as required in late February. The plants can then be brought into strong growth in early spring by being moved into a warmer position, but must be hardened off thoroughly before going out into the garden in May.

Most of us enjoy raising plants from seed. There is something magical about the process. In it is all the mystery of springtime and rebirth. Within the dry seed coat is the embryo, the germ of life, and concentrated food to nourish the plant during germination.

All that the seed needs to bring it to life is moisture, air and warmth. The moisture of the soil penetrates the case and the seed starts to swell. A tiny rootlet pushes down into the earth and a miniature shoot pushes up towards the light. The food contained within the seed is drawn on by the developing seedling.

At the same time, the roots begin to absorb chemicals from the soil and the unfolding leaves draw light from the sun and oxygen from the air, the raw chemicals being converted into sugar, starch and other products to help the plant to grow. All this is impossible without the right soil conditions.

It is useless sowing seeds until the soil has warmed up with the spring sunshine. Few seeds germinate well at a temperature of less than 13°C (55°F). The soil must be crumbly and well aerated. As gardeners say, there must be a good tilth. Seeds should not be sown when the ground is too wet and sticky, otherwise they rot. On the other hand, if the soil is as dry as dust, seeds have little chance to germinate. Choose a day when the soil will just crumble in your hand, preferably when light rain is forecast. Then the seed will have the necessary moisture to bring it to life. If rain does not fall you will need to water the rows with a fine-rosed can or, in the case of a wide area under seed, such as a lawn, with a sprinkler or a hose with a fine spray attachment.

The depth at which seeds should be sown differs; seed packets usually state the exact depth necessary. With home-saved seed a rough guide is to sow at a depth twice that of the broadest part of the seed. Tiny seeds need only be covered with a light scattering of soil.

Some soils are apt to cake and form a hard crust on the surface, which does not give seedlings a good chance. If your soil is like this, it is a good plan to spread a little granulated peat over the surface and rake it well in before sowing. To do your seedlings extra well, superphosphate or steamed bone flour may be raked in at 28 g to the sq m (1 oz to the sq yd) about seven to ten days before sowing.

When growing vegetables that will remain where they are sown and not be transplanted, you should mix rotted manure or compost with the bottom spit of soil when doing the preparatory dig in winter to feed the plants as they grow.

Some vegetables, and all perennial flowers, are sown in seed-beds, to be planted out later in the summer. The seed-bed should be out of the full sun, yet not too wet. Too wet a site would lead to damping off of the seedlings and would also encourage slugs. Semi-shade out of the full midday sun is ideal. The soil of the seed-bed should be well-drained, gritty, friable and yet moist. Peat will help you to get just the right conditions. On very sticky ground it is a good plan to make a slightly raised seed-bed with a layer of ashes beneath the friable soil.

Seeds should always be sown thinly. Sowing too thickly leads to cramping and impoverishment of the seedlings after germination. It also means a lot of work in the way of thinning out. Large seeds, like peas and beans, may be sown separately at the proper distance apart, and this will be found to give by far the best results. Tiny seeds may be sown from a sugar dredger or a cocoa tin with holes punched in the lid. Some people mix the seed with sand to ensure sowing thinly. I find, however, that careful sowing – a pinch at a time from the seed packet – usually gives the desired result. With medium-sized seed, such as that of delphiniums and scarlet flax, it is quite simple to sow each seed separately, and in the end this proves well worth the extra trouble and time.

Most small seeds are sown in drills, shallow lines drawn out carefully in the soil with the end of the rake. Larger seeds, such as peas, will do well sown criss-cross in a drill 15 cm (6 in) wide which is usually taken out with the spade. In the case of deep drills the soil is drawn back into position with the rake after sowing. With small seeds, sown just under the surface, I like to scatter the soil by hand over the seed drills. This avoids disturbing the newly sown seed. If your soil is wet or cold the seed may be covered by sand (not from the seashore). On light soils, moistened, fine peat is best.

Fungus troubles and depredations by the birds may be warded off by dressing the seeds with proprietary compounds, but except for very special seeds I hardly think this is worth the trouble. Black cotton stretched over the rows is quite an effective way of keeping off the birds, and, provided the seed-bed has been prepared properly, fungus diseases will not be a problem.

Hardy seeds are sown in March or April, according to the season. Half-hardy seeds are sown either indoors in February or in the open ground in May. Indoor sowings should be made in flat seed-boxes or in seed-pans. A special compost such as the John Innes seed compost should be used. Pelleted seeds are more expensive but they are easy to handle and tend to give more certain results (see Chapter Fourteen).

Another good method of increasing your stock of plants is by taking cuttings. Some cuttings, such as those of herbaceous perennials – delphiniums, phloxes and chrysanthemums, for example – are taken in spring when strong growth begins. Other plants such as the anchusa and Oriental poppy are increased by means of root cuttings in late winter, pieces of root being cut up and inserted vertically in pots in sandy compost in slight heat. The lower end of the root should be cut slanting, to differentiate it from the top end, and the cutting can then be inserted the right way up without difficulty.

Shrub cuttings are of two kinds, hardwood and softwood. The hardwood cuttings consist of ripened wood cut from the current year's shoots and inserted in the open ground from September onwards. As a general rule these should be about 23 cm (9 in) long, cut just below a leaf joint. The lower leaves are removed and the cuttings should then be laid in a slanting trench (i.e. with one slightly slanting side against which the cuttings can be leant) with 15 cm (6 in) of their length below ground.

Softwood cuttings consist of the tips of new shoots, which are still soft, about 7·5 or 10 cm (3 or 4 in) long. They can be taken any time between early June and late August, and will really need a frame. However, this need not be as expensive as it sounds. I have made many a useful cuttings frame from a box with the bottom knocked out, the sides cut to allow it to slope gently forwards, and with a sheet of glass cut to fit tightly over the top, as described earlier. Such a frame should stand in a fairly sheltered spot in the garden. If the sun reaches it, the cuttings will strike more quickly, but you must be prepared to shade the frame with brown paper during hot sunshine.

Most shrubs root best in a mixture of peat, sand and good loam. I break up the soil at the bottom of the frame and add a fine compost of this mixture to form the top 5 or 7·5 cm (2 or 3 in) of rooting material in the frame. Remove the lowest pair of leaves from the cutting before inserting, and water the soil well first, always keeping it moist. Each morning you will need to raise the glass and wipe off condensed moisture from the inside.

The frame is kept closed for a month or six weeks until the cuttings are rooted and growing well. Then the glass is raised, admitting more air each day, until finally it is removed altogether, being replaced only in autumn, at night, or when frost is threatened. For the first winter the cuttings will remain in the frame. Next spring you may plant them out, either in their permanent situations or in nursery beds.

What kind of cuttings do best in such a frame? Well, I have been successful with fuchsias, hydrangeas, dwarf rhododendrons and azaleas, rosemary, old-fashioned roses, escallonias, veronicas, viburnums, thymes and such rare shrubs as the Chilean lantern tree – *Crinodendron hookeranum* – which is only safely hardy on the west and south-west coasts. Side shoots, 7·5 or 10 cm (3 or 4 in) long, with a heel, seem to give the best results. Some shrubs such as mock oranges, laburnums, forsythias and the tougher hardy shrubs do better when cuttings of ripened wood are taken in autumn as described earlier.

Cuttings of heliotrope, fuchsias, pelargoniums, hydrangeas, penstemons and calceolarias are usually taken in August. Choose short-jointed, non-flowering young shoots and cut immediately below the joint, removing the lower one or two leaves. Then set the cuttings individually around the edge of a well-crocked pot filled preferably with John Innes cuttings compost (though potting No. 1 will do) and covered with a thin layer of sand. Alternatively the heliotrope, penstemon and calceolaria cuttings may be set in boxes, the cuttings spaced 7·5 cm (3 in) apart. Cuttings of this type can be placed in the cold frame to root, and may be over-wintered there provided the frame is well sacked-up during frosty weather. Whenever possible during the day, the glass must be raised a little to let in air.

Many people enjoy growing roses from cuttings, and to my mind this is quite a good practice. Roses so grown are 'on their own roots'. That is, they are not grafted, and so cannot send up suckers of alien stock. They may take a year or two to become established, but once away they grow strongly and make very good bushes. Some of my best roses have been grown from cuttings.

The time to take rose cuttings is late September or early October. Choose new shoots which have not flowered and make the cuttings about 23–30 cm (9–12 in) long, removing all the leaves except the top two or three. The cuttings can be taken with or without a heel of older wood; if without a heel a clean cut should be made, as with any cutting, just below a leaf joint.

Prepare a narrow slanting trench about 30 cm (1 ft) deep and line the bottom with coarse sand. Insert the cutting, leaving only the top 10 cm (4 in) or so above ground. Keep well watered and do not attempt to plant out your young rose bushes until the second autumn from striking.

Pelargoniums are popular subjects which will strike easily in summer. These do not need a 'heel'. Select strong growths of side shoots about 10 cm (4 in) long and cut through cleanly just below a node or 'joint'. Leave the shoots for twelve hours to wilt and form a callus.

Then insert them round the side of 12-cm (5-in) pots, four or five to a pot, in a mixture of sandy, loamy compost. Put blown-up polythene bags over them, fastened with a rubber band, and keep the pots of cuttings indoors and moist. By next spring you should have well-rooted young plants to plant out when frost danger is past.

Some people are successful at striking cuttings in water. The shoots are placed in an old milk bottle or deep jar, a little charcoal is put at the bottom to keep the water fresh, and the vessel is filled with water which should never be changed. Instead the level is kept topped up. After six or seven weeks roots may appear. As soon as the shoot has formed good roots, it is carefully removed from the water and planted out of doors in good soil in a shady place.

CHAPTER SIX

Backyard into silk purse

Before starting the conversion of a typical backyard into a well laid-out garden it is necessary to decide which parts of the existing bricks or paving should be retained. Then follows the redesigning of the plot and the rearrangement of the beds.

If there is an existing tree, it might well be wise to decide to retain it, perhaps enhancing it with a raised bed surround as suggested in Chapter Three. Alternatively one might decide merely to expose the soil around the bole. Then if moist peat or rotted compost is added it can be used as a home for crocus species, snowdrops, winter aconites and grape hyacinths, sowing dwarf nasturtium seeds among their yellowing foliage to take over the summer display. If the site is sunny, the annual *Convolvulus* 'Royal Ensign' would be an attractive alternative, but the flowers of this plant will not open in shade. Unless the tree is a fruit-bearer – apple, plum or pear – you may decide to remove or shorten some of the branches in order to let in more light and air.

Where an established tree has seriously robbed the ground, drying the soil and excluding light, the affected area may have to be planted with such dry shade 'toughies' as the periwinkles, *Vinca major* and *V. minor* (not forgetting the elegant, golden variegated form of *V. major*); dry-soil ferns such as the hart's tongue and the oak fern; hypericums, of which not only the invasive *H. calycinum* might be tried but also *H. olympicum*, the rock garden species with the sea-green leaves, and 'Hidcote' (which if sheared after flowering will make a compact mounded bush of about 60 × 60 cm (2 × 2 ft); *Polygonum vaccinifolium*; *Ajuga reptans* 'Variegata'; and epimediums.

Any sunny areas should be allocated for sitting out space, for a small pool if desired, or for herbs, roses, herbaceous sun-lovers, and grey- or silver-foliaged plants. Window-boxes and containers may also be used, filled with bedding plants in season to add gaiety to the immediate surroundings of the house and to the sitting out area.

Elderly people, the disabled, or sufferers from rheumatism or high blood pressure, who should avoid too much bending, might benefit from having most of the beds raised to a more convenient level. In any backyard garden the addition of some raised beds, whether of flowers, shrubs or grass, will add interest and consequence to the design, and for this reason at least one raised area, even if it is only to be in the form of a large, brick-built flower box, should be considered wherever possible. In a too shady garden, surrounded by high walls, raised beds will help matters also by bringing the plants nearer the light.

Raised beds are not difficult to make, and the surplus bricks or paving taken from areas newly designated as growing space will probably be already to hand as walling material. Such retaining walls will be more permanent and satisfactory if built on a solid foundation. So, unless you are keeping part of the original paving for the purpose or constructing the retaining wall on the margin of an existing solid path, it is as well to remove 15 cm (6 in) of soil and to set in a foundation of concrete 15 cm (6 in) wide and 10 cm (4 in) deep. The concrete should consist of 1 part cement, 2 parts sand and 4 parts gravel (parts by volume). The actual concrete bedding should always be a little wider than are the bricks. Consolidate the concrete by ramming it with a baulk of timber. Then use a spirit level to check that it is perfectly flat. It is impossible to build satisfactorily on an uneven surface.

Once the concrete has set, you can start to build your wall, using a mixture of 1 part cement to 3 parts sand as a mortar. Spread a layer of mortar nearly as wide as the bricks and about 1 m (3–4 ft) long. Work the top of the trowel down the centre of the mortar, and tap the end brick well down onto it. Next lay the first brick at the other end. Stretch a guide line along the upper edge of the bricks. Then spread a little mortar onto the end of the next brick and place it against the first. Continue building from each end in turn, setting any blocks that may need to be cut to fit in towards the centre, where they will be less noticeable. As you work, keep checking that the wall is rising vertically. These same principles also apply to the building of flower boxes.

Dry stone walls, in which earth is used in place of mortar, can be very effective. They should be built on the same lines as walls of bricks, except that they should lean back with a slight batter, so as to retain better the weight of earth that they are to contain. An occasional stone should be set end on, into the earth bank, in order to give greater strength to the barrier. Such walls may also be built back to back with a core of earth in the middle; a 30-cm (1-ft) width of earth will enable rock plants or dwarf hedging material such as lavender, rosemary, cistus or hardy fuchsias to be set on top.

For the raised bed 60–75 cm (2–2½ ft) will usually be found to be the best height, although if you are making a raised lawn a height of 15–30 cm (6–12 in) will be sufficient to give the interest of a different level without presenting too much of a problem in lifting the mower to the required height. In our small garden we find the highly portable, lightweight, electric, Black and Decker grass-cutter entirely suitable.

After the containing walls have been built, the cement should be allowed to set really hard for at least a week before the bed is filled with soil. If you are going to use the raised bed to grow alpines or bedding plants, the bottom foot can be filled with rubble or drainage material. You will then only need to import good soil for the top spit. On the other hand, if shrubs or roses are to be grown, it will be worth filling up the whole box with fertile topsoil. If you intend using old soil excavated from elsewhere in the garden – perhaps to make room for a pool – you should interlace it liberally with rotted compost, manure or peat, treat it with lime to offset the sourness of the stagnant worn-out soil, and even so top it up, yearly if possible, with fresh earth.

Raised beds filled with an acid-reacting compost make good homes for lime-hating plants if your garden soil is alkaline. For these to succeed, you should obtain a load of lime-free soil and mix it well with a coarse grade of moist peat. In such a bed, dwarf rhododendrons and evergreen azaleas will be very happy. Some of them may be relied on to give a scattering of bloom in autumn in addition to their late spring and early summer display, and one might interplant or edge the bed with summer- and winter-flowering heaths to ensure that the area is kept colourful throughout the year. To prevent lime contamination, a sheet of heavy-duty black polythene should be placed over the base before the bed is filled with lime-free compost.

Raised beds can be rendered even more pleasing to the eye if alpine carpeting plants are set close to the edge where they can grow forward and pour down in mats to drape the wall. Alpine phloxes, lithospermums, dianthus, prostrate rosemary, *Gypsophila reptans*, *Veronica prostrata* and, in mild coastal areas, succulent daisies of the lampranthus (mesembryanthemum) type might be used, in addition to the more common aubrietas and alyssums, of which last the primrose and the buff forms might be chosen to add variety to the more usual mustard.

Most backyards are either long and narrow or else severely rectangular. To add interest and a sense of design, circular and triangular shapes might be introduced in the form of grass or flower beds. It helps, too, where possible, to incorporate a diagonal or semi-diagonal path – perhaps of staggered paving. Alternatively, semi-circular or horseshoe beds would help.

If limiting the amount of conversion work is all-important, the basic oblong could be rendered more interesting by the positioning of a formal off-centre pool or bed, the addition of a simply made raised flower box at one side of the garden, and the provision of a sitting out area at the end which gets the most sunshine. A broad bed at one side of the garden and a much narrower one at the other side also serves to lessen the severity and creates an illusion of greater width.

Many tiny gardens are too small to include a tree, but wherever possible the planting of a single specimen should be considered – even if it be only a tree-type shrub.

By its placing a small tree will help to offset too symmetrical a look, and by its height it will bring in a new dimension. Such a little tree might be set towards the far corner of the plot. It could, for screenage purposes, have an arbour built around it – in which case its head should protrude above the cross-beams of the top – or it might be positioned slightly off-centre, and nearer the house, near the wall on the opposite side of the garden to the sitting out arbour.

Only very small trees should be considered. Ideal subjects are the frilly 'Musical Comedy' apricot, *Prunus* × *blireana*, which bears its fragrant rose-pink flowers in April, followed by leaves of coppery purple; *Styrax japonica*, the summer Snowdrop tree, which is suitable only for acid soils; *Prunus* 'Amanogawa', the maypole cherry, so strictly upright that it occupies a space only 60 cm (2 ft) square; and *Amelanchier laevis*, which is less likely to sucker than *A. lamarchii* and can easily be trained to a single stem, this tree being particularly attractive in May when the fragrant white blossom mingles with the delicate pink of the young leaves. The upright *Laburnum* 'Vossii' with its extra long racemes might also be chosen, as careful nipping back of any outward-facing shoots that threaten to over-reach will keep it well within its allotted space. The silver weeping pear, *Pyrus salicifolia pendula*, is a beautiful small tree which does not resent pruning and is characterful enough to use as the main focal point of a tiny garden.

A striking effect, to give the aspect of a weeping tree on a shorter stem, can be obtained if *Wistaria floribunda* 'Macrobotrys' is standard-trained. This can be quite easily achieved by setting it against a $1\frac{1}{2}$-m (5-ft) post at planting time and tying in the main stem to the post. The side shoots should be rigidly removed until the desired height is reached. The head is then built up by pinching back the main side shoots to six or seven buds and then nipping back all laterals on these side shoots to two buds. Within a few years a most delightful and characterful gnarled Japanese-looking tree will be obtained. For the maximum impact it should be planted beside a pool – preferably to leeward so that the falling leaves are blown clear of the water. Alternatively the pool can be netted in the autumn when the leaves begin to drop. The wistaria would be almost equally effective if planted on the edge of a cobbled circle, square or triangle on which decorative tubs or other containers were set, filled with low-growing or bedding plants. Daffodils, hyacinths, or dwarf double tulips for spring might precede ivy-leaved pelargoniums, petunias or stocks for summer. Dwarf Japanese maples such as the cut-leaved, bronze-foliaged *Acer palmatum* 'Dissectum' would be equally good in such a position.

The sorbus family succeeds in most town gardens and there are two species and one hybrid which are sufficiently restricted in growth to be used as specimens in the backyard garden. They are large-fruited *S. scopulina*, with berries of sealing wax red, which makes a tall, columnar shrub or small upright tree; its hybrid off-spring, the orange-fruited 'Signalman', which was raised by Hillier's of Winchester; and the white-berried *S. cashmiriana*, which has quite large pinkish blossoms in attractive sprays in May. *S. cashmiriana* is similar in growth to *S. scopulina*.

The enthusiastic plant lover in the southern or western half of the country might consider *Eucryphia* × *nymansensis* as a subject for tiny garden planting. The cultivar 'Nymansay' is usually narrowly cylindrical in growth, and its conspicuously stamened, white, rose-of-sharon-like flowers are shown off well by dark, evergreen foliage. Should this tree become too tall, as occasionally happens in the course of fifteen years or so, it is not too difficult a matter to remove the top.

Conifers, as a whole, do not do well in most town gardens. Only the deciduous conifers really succeed and their winter aspect is not sufficiently pleasing to warrant their inclusion in a very small plot. However the columnar form of *Ginkgo biloba*, with leaves like a maiden hair fern, is worth excepting. This form is known as 'Fastigiata'. Tolerant of atmospheric pollution, it is both beautiful and useful, and it, too, can be topped if it grows too tall.

Remembering the general poverty of soil in most backyard gardens, special care should be taken when preparing the planting site for a tree. Ideally, a 90-cm (3-ft) cube should be broken up and a 10-cm (4-ft) layer of manure sandwiched between the top and bottom spits. The top spit should be further conditioned by the incorporation of moss peat or hop manure. A handful of bonemeal will also be found beneficial except in the case of the calcifuge subjects.

Shade in the tiny garden is not an insurmountable problem. There is a wide range of shade-tolerant plants of all types, in addition to those which actually need shade. Even dry shade is not too difficult so long as moist peat is incorporated into the planting sites and watering is conscientiously carried out. Shade-lovers such as ferns are effective along with trilliums, lily-of-the-valley, primulas, meconopses and hellebores, but they *must* be kept moist. Solomon's seal, epimediums and tiarella will also do well in shady places.

Shade beneath trees where starlings roost is another, and much more difficult, matter. Here, the acidity of the birds' droppings burns the plants beneath. Rain drip aggravates the condition, and only ivies and *Hypericum calycinum* will really give satisfaction. But even with this problem, one need not despair. There are some attractively variegated ivies which would survive, and one might experiment by including a few bulbs among them. One might also surround the difficult area with cobbles or stone paving on which tubs or other containers may stand. Then a 'disaster region' would be turned into a good garden asset.

The following plants are shade-tolerant to varying degrees.
Others are discussed in Chapter Nine.

SHRUBS

Camellia japonica cultivars
Elaeagnus
Fatsia japonica
Hedera helix 'Arborescens' (tree
    ivy)
Hydrangea

Hypericum
Holly
Magnolia
Mahonia
Skimmia

GROUND-COVERING PLANTS

Vinca major and *V. minor* (the
    periwinkles, in their various
    forms)
Ferns
Helleborus
Hosta

Hypericum
Polygonatum
Primula
Tiarella
Trillium

CLIMBERS

Hydrangea petiolaris
Lonicera
Parthenocissus henryana (a prettily
    variegated 'vine')

Actinidia chinensis
Rosa 'Mermaid'

BEDDING PLANTS

Begonia
Impatiens

Nicotiana

Many bulbs are shade-tolerant, including *Camassia esculenta*,
chionodoxa, crocus, cyclamen, eranthis (winter aconite), erythronium, fritillaria, galanthus (snowdrop), ipheion (tritellia), *Iris
histrioides* and *I. reticulata*, muscari (grape hyacinth), leucojum (snowflake) and many narcissi (dwarf and large), scillas and Spanish bluebells.

Magnolias undoubtedly do well in town gardens but the problem
is to find any small enough in growth for the backyard garden. Room
may perhaps be found for *M. stellata*, the early Japanese species with
its pretty, star-petalled flowers. It prefers an acid soil. Of the later

M. × *soulangiana* cultivars, with their typical goblet cups, we find 'Picture' vigorous, yet erect enough in habit to be easily accommodated in a very restricted space, if one rigorously removes any shoots encroaching beyond its allotted circumference. Flowering when young, the outsides of its chalices are richly stained with purple. This cultivar blooms in May and carries a few flowers in autumn also. Later to bloom, usually in June, the weaker-growing *M. liliiflora* in its cultivar 'Nigra' is also compact enough for the purpose. Deeper in colour than 'Picture', this magnolia is inclined to do poorly on limy soils, whereas 'Picture' is to some degree lime-tolerant. Both will grow in clay.

In addition to one or two small trees, the larger backyard garden will probably be able to offer homes to a selection of small shrubs. These should be chosen as far as possible to cover the main seasons of the year, at the same time trying to associate together those that offer pleasing colour combinations. For instance, the misty blue caryopteris is at its most effective when grouped with purple-leaved *Berberis thunbergii* 'Atropurpurea Nana' and the coppery apricot *Potentilla* 'Tangerine'.

A descriptive list of shrubs together with sizes will be found in Chapter Ten. Heathers, taking up as they do very little space, furnishing the garden throughout the year, and offering a wide season of floral interest, are double *plus* plants for the tiny garden. The winter-flowering varieties are lime-tolerant, as to some extent are the Cornish *Erica vagans* cultivars. The callunas and bell heathers should, however, be grown in raised beds of lime-free soil where the general growing medium of the garden is alkaline, except for *E. carnea* and its cultivars.

Like trees, shrubs must be offered a good growing compost. Whether in the shrub border or in individual sites, the soil should be changed to a 60-cm (2-ft) depth, or – where this is not possible – existing soil should be broken up to two spades' depth and generous quantities of rotted garden compost, manure and coarse, moist peat incorporated.

For herbaceous plants, it will be sufficient to break up the bottom strata and dig the enlivening humus into the top spit. Because in a tiny space it is important to choose only the best, a list of compact herbaceous species and varieties that can be relied on for their floral performance will be found in Chapter Eleven.

In these days of garden centres, one may often be tempted by the display of roses, herbaceous plants and shrubs already in bloom. This type of instant gardening can be quite satisfactory if you buy good plants and look after them well. Each plant should be well established in its container and yet not have been there long enough to have rooted through into the gravel or peat below. It is a good test to pick the plant up by its foliage or main stem: if it lifts easily yet does not come out of the container, it should be safe to buy.

Once you get it home strip off the plastic film or tap it out of the drum. If it has been grown in a metal container, get the nursery to slit it down before you take it away. Prepare a hole large enough to contain it with the top of the soil ball about 1·2 cm ($\frac{1}{2}$ in) below soil level. Pack good soil laced with peat around it and water well. It will be necessary to keep a watch throughout the season to ensure it does not dry out before the roots have found their way into the surrounding soil. If planted between April and October, this could mean regular watering for several weeks. In fact, it should never be allowed to dry out completely during the first summer.

CHAPTER SEVEN

Tiny front gardens

Planning a front garden depends very much on the amount of space one has to deal with. In the scope of this chapter, we shall consider pocket-handkerchief plots from $4\frac{1}{2} \times 6$ m (15×20 ft) down to the 2- or $2\frac{1}{2}$-m (6- or 8-ft) strip flanking the steps, that is the bonus some terraced town houses have over those whose front doors open direct onto the pavement.

With the larger plots it is possible to use some sort of basic design. Always the purpose should be to detract from the ordinariness of the square or oblong shape. In most front gardens the gate will be already in position and the path will take the logical and shortest route – in a direct line to the front door leaving only a small square for gardening operations.

Two main factors will then govern the plan for this remaining area: a. the aspect, whether it is sunny or shaded, windswept or enclosed, and b. whether the owner wants to use the area intensively to pursue his hobby, or whether the main requirement is that it should be neat and easily maintained and set off the house to the best advantage.

For those who really enjoy gardening, one of the best solutions I have seen was the creation of a small, round lawn, so limited in area that it was possible for the turf always to be immaculate. This was immediately surrounded by a circle of cobbles, perhaps a foot in width. The rest of the space between the lawn and the paths was then devoted to flower gardening of the intensive cottage type. The planting was graded, with small rock plants spilling over the cobbled circle and also softening the edges of the paths. Then by a gradation of small and less small bulbs, pansies, stocks, primulas and antirrhinums, an irregular central ridge was formed by such taller growers as lupins, peonies, pyrethrums and rudbeckias. Lilac, lavender, forsythia, rosemary and flowering currant grew against the roadside railings to give additional height and to make a screen without cutting off too much of the light. This particular garden faced south, but a similar effect could be achieved in a more sunless aspect by using Japanese anemones, foxgloves, trilliums, primulas, hostas, ferns, Solomon's seal and lilies-of-the-valley.

More formal treatment could be given to a similar garden facing south, west or east, by instituting a planting of Senecio cineraria 'White Diamond' and allowing its silver-white leaves to act as a background for scarlet roses, scarlet dwarf dahlias, scarlet gladioli and blood-red Begonia semperflorens. Mounds of pink and lavender fuchsias would have a softening effect. In spring the silver senecio leaves could offer an attractive background to blood-red and flame-coloured wallflowers, interspersed with tulips in scarlet and black. In cold areas the senecio would not be winter-hardy, but in much of the south and west it would survive as a permanent planting. A softer colour scheme of shades of pink and mauve would be equally effective, or one might utilize the silver of the senecio to set off plantings of white and yellow to give a permanently sunny effect. (See Chapter Nine for further suggestions for this kind of scheme.)

A more labour-saving scheme using fewer plants might consist of formal paving, varied in texture by cobbled panels, on which could be set containers of bulbs or bedding plants. Such a scheme might incorporate a raised, boxed-in border of small shrubs, culminating in a slightly larger tree-type shrub of visual impact such as one of the Japanese maples, or Mahonia japonica, near the gate. Alternatively the paved area might feature a small tree set in a square or circle of grass with two or three containers placed on the paving for colour.

One might create a Japanese effect by incorporating a pebble bed in the paving, setting on it two or three weathered boulders of interesting shape, and limiting the planting to a strategically placed clump of the tall, striped grass, Miscanthus sinensis 'Zebrinus', near which might be stood a container-grown Bonsai tree.

Open-plan front gardens present more of a problem. Here, with invading children and dogs, it is useless to attempt much in the way of cultivation. Better to concentrate on an effect which blends with the other gardens, whether of turf or paving, perhaps adding an informal island bed of shrubs based on the prickly Berberis thunbergii atropurpurea, the equally prickly Juniperus horizontalis 'Douglasii' (which should succeed in these more open conditions), and the ultra-tough Mahonia aquifolium, which adds to the attraction of its holly-like leaflets the charm of lemon-yellow flowers in early spring.

For a narrower strip of town garden protected by railings one can be more selective. One can add, also, to the planting area by using window-boxes and wall pots which can be kept filled with a seasonal succession of bloom. For the boxes, one might choose the winter-flowering *Erica carnea* heaths, interplanted with *greigii* tulip hybrids for spring. These might be followed by a scheme of trailing ivy-leaf and upright zonal pelargoniums in lavender, pink and white. Or one could decide on the extravagance of blue hydrangeas, interplanted with pink, ivy-leaved pelargoniums. Less expensively, one might choose Cambridge blue lobelia with mixed pink and white antirrhinums; or deep blue lobelia, dwarf orange French marigolds and trailing 'Golden Gleam' nasturtiums. Apart from consideration of cost, one's choice must be guided by the colour scheme of the house and also by its aspects. Petunias, begonias and ivy-leaved pelargoniums will put up a good show, in even a north-facing situation.

Variegated ivies and ferns might be used for the wall pots, or one might decide on flowering plants. In this case the ivy-leaved pelargonium might again be the best choice, as one wants a subject which will trail gracefully. Trailing tuberous begonias would also be good, as would such fuchsias as 'Alice Hofman' and 'Marinka'.

For permanent planting, one might add the luxury of a camellia accompanied by the exotic-looking rhododendron 'Lady Chamberlain' with its apricot and yellow hanging trumpets and small blue-green oval leaves. Both these subjects need lime-free soil, but for such a small area it should be possible to make a raised bed of suitable compost or else to grow them in containers. They might be accompanied by a planting of lilies, either in tubs or in the ground. The lilies could be chosen to cover a long season, from the early yellow 'Destiny' with its upright candelabras, through the trumpets of the speciosums to the late-flowering glory of the giant auratums. Among them, one might place the tall *Galtonia candicans*, the white Cape hyacinth, with its lily-like bells. Given a raised bed in sun, *Nerine bowdenii* would also be easy, and the crimped beauty of its glowing pink trumpets would add greatly to the autumn scene. Less demanding, and continuous in flower from late October into the depth of winter, are the schizostylis, of which the crimson type and the soft pink 'Viscountess Byng' are the most reliable. They are like tiny gladioli and will do well in any reasonably sunny spot, provided they are given water during the growing season.

In the south and west, wherever a spot of poor soil is vacant against a sunny wall, the Algerian *Iris unguicularis* (syn. *I. stylosa*) should be planted for the charm of its delicate lavender blossoms which unfold from tight-rolled, umbrella-like fawn buds in any mild spells throughout the winter. They are wonderfully cheering to pick in bud and they open in the warmth of the sitting room during a winter's evening reading or watching the television.

For a key position at the front of the house the greatest possible use should be made of hardy bulbs. They are easy to grow and will give a certain return – even if after their first season of display one lifts them and places them in the backyard garden or donates them to country-dwelling friends who will perhaps reciprocate with gifts of bedding plants or fruit.

In towns, crocuses are usually more likely to be successful than they are in the country, where they are subject to the raids of field mice and voles. Should the town mice show a tendency to enjoy a diet of crocus corms they may be discouraged by shoots of holly and prickly berberis set in the ground to encircle each group. From the early 'Golden Bunch' rock garden crocuses through the amethyst and lavender 'Tommies' – *Crocus tomasinianus* – to the fat yellows, striped varieties and purples of the Dutch hybrids, crocuses give a great deal of pleasure in bringing an early breath of spring to town gardens. In the formal front garden they can be followed by bedding hyacinths and a little later by the low-growing *greigii* and *kaufmanniana* tulip hybrids or the stocky, early double tulips which are not tall enough to catch the wind. Later the more leggy Mendels and Darwins might grow amidst the shelter of Brompton stocks or wallflowers which would help to protect their stems. Even the Spanish bluebell – now officially known as *Endymion* – should not be overlooked, especially in its charming white variety. Its earlier, near-relations, the scillas and puschkinias, too, should be tucked into every possible corner along with the best of the *Iris reticulata* hybrids, like 'Joyce', and the brilliant blue or white muscari. Taking up, as they do, so little room, bulbs are a great blessing to the owners of tiny gardens.

Alpine edgings can greatly improve the appearance of both front and back gardens. Tough little rock plants that will spread over the retaining bricks, or spill onto the paths, not only soften a harsh outline but add greatly to the colour and interest of the garden as a whole.

Some of the best plants for the purpose are *Campanula carpatica* and the smaller *pusilla*, alpine phloxes such as 'Eva', aubrieta (which should be clipped hard back after flowering so that it remains neat and compact), thrift, helianthemums (which should also be sheared back when their rock rose blooms are over), sedums such as 'Coral Carpet', and the various forms of alpine dianthus.

CHAPTER EIGHT

Basements and roofs

Basement area gardens are among the most difficult to deal with, suffering as they do from shortage of light and stagnation of air. They tend also to suffer from waterlogging, and general sourness of the soil. Moreover, plants grown at such a low level tend to become leggy and poor-looking as they struggle to reach the light.

Lack of light is a severe drawback, and one that should be counteracted by making the most of all available reflecting surfaces, distempering or painting the walls white or cream.

Waterlogging can be offset to some extent by the planting of water-greedy permanent plants such as hydrangeas. These will inevitably thrust up longer than usual stems in order to reach the light, so to offset this one might make a virtue of necessity and choose to plant the elegant-leaved and more subtle-flowered *Hydrangea sargentiana* or *H. villosa*, in which legginess will only serve to bring their best features nearer the height at which they can most conveniently be appreciated. The so-called 'dwarf' bamboo, *Arundinaria nitida*, which reaches a height of nearly 2 m (6 ft) or more, might also be planted, together with rodgersias and *Ligularia clivorum*. It will not matter whether these last two genera flower or not, as their luxuriant foliage is sufficient beauty and both are efficient at mopping up surplus moisture. *Rodgersia tabularis* with its great, plate-like leaves is particularly grateful for the shady conditions of a basement area. Beautiful too, is the bronzy-leaved *R. podophylla* with palmate leaves of which each leaflet is shaped like a duck's webbed foot. Both species, when they flower, throw up white plumes like those of an astilbe. Zebra Grass – *Miscanthus sinensis* 'Zebrinus' – will also help to absorb the moisture, and in basement conditions will often throw up its leaves to a height of 2 m (6–7 ft).

Unfortunately the rodgersias and the grass die to the ground in the winter so one will have to take thought for off-season interest by planting a background of evergreen creepers to drape the walls. The variegated ivies such as the large-leaved *Hedera colchica* 'Dentata Variegata', the smaller *Hedera helix* 'Gold Heart', 'Glacier' with its grey and white colouration and 'Silver Queen' will all be acceptable. For winter ground cover, the cream and green variegated form of the larger periwinkle, *Vinca major* 'Variegata', will send out its elegant trails.

In such conditions *Aralia elata* might be grown, either in the type or in the gold or cream variegated forms known as 'Aureovariegata' and 'Variegata' respectively. It will not matter unduly if they become drawn up, as it will merely serve to bring their beautiful foliage to a higher level. Philadelphus also does well in wet soils, as does the variegated *Weigela florida* 'Variegata'. The white, scented blossoms of the philadelphus and the creamy variegated leaves of the weigela would be particularly appreciated in such a position.

To bring the plants nearer to the street level and the light one can make raised beds and use wall pots, in addition to constructing shelving or bracketed pot-holders, to hold plants at higher levels. In these, pendulous begonias and ivy-leaved pelargoniums might be used for summer decoration, as both these subjects flower fairly well in shade. Petunias might also be tried, and the scented nicotiana and its hybrids either set in a raised bed or at the lower level. Solomon's seal and lily-of-the-valley should give results, and I have known the early spring-flowering, tiny-trumpeted *Narcissus cyclamineus*, with its fly-away perianth; its larger and later hybrids; the dog's tooth violet, *Erythronium* 'White Beauty'; and the Spanish bluebell, succeed. With ferns and hostas, the basement area can be rendered attractive for most of the year.

Deciduous climbers, too, are suitable, such as the delicately coloured vine, *Parthenocissus henryana*, with its small, bronzy leaflets veined with cream – a variation that becomes more pronounced in semi-shade. Self-clinging when established, it may need a little gentle training in the first year or two. A Netlon panel set against the wall will take care of this. *P. henryana* has the advantage that if concrete footings militate against its being planted right against the wall, it will grow happily in a tub or trough. This makes it particularly useful for paved basement areas.

Honeysuckles will usually give a good account of themselves in semi-shade. *Lonicera periclymenum* 'Belgica' and 'Serotina', the early and late Dutch honeysuckles, will obligingly grow in tubs and

flower freely in partial shade. A hybrid, alas without scent, that prefers even full shade is the showy _L._ × _tellmanniana_, with 5-cm (2-in)
flowers of rich coppery yellow. When grown in shade, most honeysuckles flower quite well and are much more resistant to nuisance
attacks from aphis. Unlike the ivies and the parthenocissus, however,
they must have support. This may be given in the shape of plastic
mesh panelling pegged to the wall. Square mesh wooden trellis may
also be used.

Many plants which do well in damp and rather shady conditions
have white or yellow flowers – pale pink and mauve also look well,
taking on a luminosity that they lack when in full sun.

When dealing with the physical problem of the soil structure of a
basement area it is worth remembering the moisture-absorbing
properties of peat. As coarse a grade of peat as possible should be dug
into the soil, and this is the one occasion when it need not be
moistened before use.

Roof gardening is another facet of town gardening that has its
own particular problems. Obviously the first requirement when
embarking on the making of a roof garden is to be sure that the roof
will bear the weight of the containers, garden furniture, soil and
beds. Given this, fascinating tiny gardens can often be made on the
roofs of flats or offices blocks, or even on the leaded spaces that are
sometimes to be found connecting the roofs of two buildings.

Often grass will flourish on a city roof, and the laying of a tiny
lawn necessitates only the construction of a 23-cm (9-in) raised bed.
Fine ashes 7·5 cm (3 in) deep should be put down for drainage
purposes, and the top 15 cm (6 in) be composed of a fine grade of
moist peat mixed with loam. Bedding plants and bulbs may be grown
in raised brick flower boxes or planted in movable troughs and pots.
Where the roof is covered with asphalt, it is a good plan to lay paving
for the paths, forming the beds by building small walls in which to
contain the soil, with adequate drainage in the form of broken clay
pots, etc. The beds should, of course, be kept as near as possible to the
bearing walls in order to keep the weight off the centre. Reconstituted stone paving of less than $2\frac{1}{2}$ cm (1 in) thick can be purchased,
and this will go a long way towards solving the question of weight.

Sometimes wind can be a problem, but city roofs are often
surprisingly protected. Sometimes the building out of a room as an
extension to a small house results in the availability of a flat roof on
which a garden can be made. Chimney breasting offers a home for

climbers, and any adjacent walls can be covered with trellis and used for the training of roses and clematis. Pelargoniums often do well in roof gardens, sometimes surviving the winter, due to good air drainage and plenty of sun-ripening for their stems. Even if one uses the roof merely as a place to sunbathe, it is worth adding a few troughs and tubs of flowers so that one has the fun of growing something to beautify the surroundings.

Roof gardeners have many problems peculiar to their own situation which must be borne in mind when their gardens are made. Chief of these is the question of weight, referred to earlier. Some roofs, particularly those of modern construction, may be quite unequal to supporting quantities of soil or paving. Soil in the flower beds or containers can increase considerably in weight during periods of heavy rain or snow. Peat weighs less than soil, and to make up a still lighter compost one might consider mixing it with vermiculite (obtainable as Micafil from builders' suppliers). Such a growing medium contains no plant foods, so fertilizers must be added before planting, and the nutriment element topped up from time to time. Balanced general garden fertilizers such as Garden Plus or Growmore contain the necessary minerals and trace elements for healthy plant growth. They can be supplemented by liquid feeds such as the sea-weed-based Maxicrop or Liquinure, administered during the growing season.

Drainage, too, plays an important part, both in keeping down weight and in the prevention of waterlogging. Most flat roofs will already have provision for the escape of surplus water, but extra care should be taken to keep these outlets free from clogging with leaves or rubbish.

The disposal of garden rubbish is in itself a problem when one gardens at roof level. One solution, used by one London roof-gardener, is the installation of a pulley, fixed to the balustrade or railings. By using about 12 m (40 ft) of stout sashcord and a meat hook, buckets of debris can be lowered to the ground floor without the necessity of trailing them through the house; it can also act as a hoist for peat and fertilizers. A compost bin in lightweight plastic, strategically placed near a wall where its potential weight strain is least, can be used for the disposal of leaves, clippings, etc., ultimately adding a valuable supply of organic fertilizer to the beds.

Wind is a hazard to most roof gardeners. Its impact can best be lessened by the use of netting or gauze, stretched to a height of

1 or 1½ m (4 or 5 ft) around the perimeter railings or balustrade. Additional netting might be slung between the chimney breastings and could be used as a support for sweetpeas or other annual climbers to disguise during the summer months. Solid wind screens offer too much resistance and lead only to disaster. Mesh has the effect of breaking up the force of the wind without causing it to swoop over and descend with increased strength on the unfortunate plants on the other side. A penetrable barrier serves to 'temper' the wind rather than to offer solid obstruction, and so is more successful in shielding plants.

CHAPTER NINE

Shade and sun

Many tiny gardens are shady. Sometimes this is due to surrounding tall buildings which cut off the light – and sometimes induce draught – and sometimes to the shade of overhanging trees, the roots of which often invade the area and rob the soil of moisture and nourishment. Whatever the cause, it need not necessarily be an occasion for despair. Some of the best and most interesting gardens have been created on shady sites.

Whatever you decide to grow, the soil will probably need attention. It will benefit from the addition of humus to improve its structure and to give nourishment to the plants. Bagged manure or well rotted compost will do both. The addition of coarse peat, which has been soaked in water for twenty-four hours before use, will help greatly to offset the dryness of the soil, as well as improving its structure. Baled peat needs to stand in a container to soak, but peat bought in a polythene bag can be soaked very easily by pouring water into the bag, and piercing holes to allow the surplus to drain away. Left overnight, the peat will absorb the moisture. Some peat, of course, is moist when sold. In any case it is well worth the trouble involved to ensure that the peat really is *wet*. It can't be too wet when you are dealing with dried-out, root-robbed soil.

Properly treated, a tree-overhung part of the garden can be turned into a place of enchantment. For autumn and early winter, plant the hybrid *Mahonia* 'Charity' with its decorative, compound leaves which bear spiny holly-like leaflets in two distinctive tiers, and are crowned by fragrant cockades of deep yellow flowers. After Christmas the later-blooming *M. japonica* with lemon-yellow blossoms can take up the tale. For a draughty site such as may occur close to a high-rise building, the April-blooming *M. aquifolium* should be substituted. All are handsome throughout the year.

To accompany the mahonias, the scented, white-flowered *Sarcococca confusa* might be planted. Oval, shining leaves and thicketing habit will give dense ground cover. Its white flowers are small but fragrant and will be borne through the later part of the winter. With it, I would set the butcher's broom – *Ruscus aculeatus* – for the beauty of its sealing-wax berries, to achieve an abundance of which a male plant should be included (sexed plants can be obtained from several reliable nurseries including Hillier's of Winchester).

Ivies and *Euonymus radicans* 'Silver Queen' might be added to complete the carpeting. Daffodils seldom establish themselves satisfactorily in town gardens, so their use is better confined to troughs or raised beds from which they may be lifted after flowering. Sometimes snowdrops can be persuaded to naturalize – or at least to survive – particularly if they are planted when in growth as described in Chapter Twelve. Bluebells, especially the native *Endymion non-scriptus*, and even the Spanish endymion, can usually be established.

In the tiny garden, one can afford to go all out for prettiness and plant the white and pink varieties of Spanish bluebell freely, either on their own, or in conjunction with the blue. Native prim-roses should succeed and are quite at home among ivy. Away from the carpeting plants, perhaps in pockets between the tree roots, the lilac-coloured Caucasian primrose, *Primula amoena* (syn. *P. altaica*), should succeed. It is charming with its smaller leaves and showy, pastel flowers. Blue primroses and polyanthus are also appealing, and could be planted either on their own or in conjunction with the yellow. One might even take a leaf from the book of Miss Jekyll, one of the great gardeners of all time, and plant a mixture of white, lemon and gold polyanthus, which would do much to lighten the gloom of an overhung, rather dark green area.

Lilies-of-the-valley and Solomon's seal are two rhizomatous subjects which flower later in the year, as spring gives way to summer. They succeed in most town gardens, but the lilies-of-the-valley do appreciate a rich, moist soil. They need generous quantities of moist peat and bagged manure, or well-made compost, if they are to give of their best.

Looking back to winter and to earliest spring, hellebores are ideal subjects for the shady garden. Of these, the Christmas rose, *Helleborus niger*, with its pristine chalices, should, like the lilies-of-the-valley, be given plenty of humus and nutriment. However, the native *H. foetidus* with its brown-rimmed, apple-green cups is undemanding and easily pleased. So are the many attractive Lenten rose hybrids which one sometimes sees listed as *H.* × *orientalis*, which species often appears in their very mixed ancestry. Taller-growing than the Christmas rose, these later-blooming hellebores bear drooping saucer-shaped flowers, varying in colour from greenish white, through white speckled with purple or rose, apple-blossom and peachy pink, to a deep claret-purple that is almost black. Whatever you may have read or been told to the contrary, they will last up to a fortnight in water, provided the stems are split for 7·5 cm (3 in) before the blossoms are plunged up to their necks in warm water. I find a witch-bowl, set on a high shelf, ideal for their arrangement. One can then look up into them and fully appreciate the loveliness of their beautifully marked cups. Later to bloom, *H. lividus* 'Corsicus', a connoisseur's plant with spiny, handsome leaves and chartreuse cups, is taller-growing and more delicate. It will do well provided you can give it a draught-free spot and either corset its stems to three small canes or provide strong twiggy sticks for its support.

Another uncommon plant with beautiful foliage is *Arum italicum pictum*, the pointed leaves of which are showily veined with cream. It needs moist leafy soil to encourage it, or it may be a few years before its leaves will be large enough to make a show. Near it, we grow the double celandine for its shining rosettes of buttercup yellow.

Attractive herbaceous plants for the shady garden include good forms of lungwort, the old soldiers and sailors of country cottage gardens. The finest of these is *Pulmonaria saccharata*, with well-spotted leaves and large crozier heads of typical rose and blue flowers. Also good is the narrow-leaved *P. angustifolia* 'Azurea', with bright blue flowers, and the early red *P. rubra*. Delightful for a sheltered spot in dappled shade is *Omphalodes cappadocica*, with neater, smaller leaves and sprays of speedwell-blue flowers.

Where damp, rich soil exists or where a moist peaty bed can be organized, the Asiatic primulas such as the robust, crimson *P. japonica*, the more refined *P. pulverulenta* 'Bartley Strain', the gold *P. heladoxa* and the apricot *P. bulleyana* will offer delightful colour from May to July, when the even taller, scented, primrose-coloured *P. sikkimensis* takes over.

Trillium grandiflorum, a bulbous plant from the North American woodland, has large, white three-petalled flowers. It is beautiful in shade, and does best in moist acid soil. One might indulge also in the luxury of the shrubby *Cornus canadensis*, the creeping dogwood. This is a deciduous carpeter which is particularly attractive in summer when its shapely leaves are studded with white dogwood flowers which in their turn give way to bright red berries. Fairly expensive to buy, it will colonize happily in partial shade provided its roots are given the moist, sandy peat and leaf-mould that it needs. *Tiarella cordifolia*, the foam flower, is like much more beautiful London pride, with fluffy white flowers above more attractive leaves.

For summer, there is the shade-loving hardy geranium, *G. wallichianum* 'Buxton's Blue', with large meadow-cranesbill, salver flowers, centred by white. Foxgloves, like the freely spotted 'Excelsior' strain, or the white, will give grace and height with their spires.

Planting a shady garden is like planting a garden that is intended to be enjoyed mainly in the evening. It is the white and pale-coloured flowers that are the most effective.

Bearing this in mind, and remembering that it will flower even against a north-facing wall, one might plant the strong-growing *Clematis montana*, giving it a wide panel of plastic mesh up which to scramble. Also suitable for a north wall is the creamy blush rose 'Mme Alfred Carrière', which flowers freely in June and again in September and is blessed with a good scent. At its foot one might plant the white form of *Campanula lactiflora*.

White honesty would add interest in spring. *Lunaria annua alba* is an annual which does best if sown the previous autumn. To its attractions it adds the charm of its silvery, moonlike seed-pods. Honesty is reliable and easy from seed, as is the pinky mauve later-flowering *Lavatera trimestris*. There is a white-flowered form of love-in-the-mist which is particularly effective, or one might sow the Thomson and Morgan 'Persian Jewels' strain of nigella, which is a mixture of several subtle shades.

One of my favourite edging plants, and one which does well in shade, is the frilly-petalled yellow and white *Limnanthes douglasii*. Children call this the scrambled egg flower, and in a shaded area it looks almost luminous and lasts in flower for many weeks.

White violas look well in shade, as do the pale lemon-yellows. White petunias, too, might be planted, along with the pale bluish varieties. Penstemons usually flower well in shade, and I love their graceful stems and curved bells which are often paler on the inside than the out.

The tall herbaceous phlox, as against the alpine type, are plants that I sometimes think are without sufficient distinction to earn a place in the tiny garden where space is at a premium. For this reason you will not find them among the recommended permanent plants in Chapter Eleven. There are, however, exceptions in the white and lavender forms.

Fuchsias generally flower well in shade. One of the hardies which in our garden is particularly good in rather deep shade is *Fuchsia magellanica* 'Alba'. In spite of its name it has flowers that are not white but blush, but which nevertheless lend an amazing grace of slender, drooping beauty to their dark corner.

The sunny site is easier to deal with than one in shade and yet at the same time it is perhaps more difficult to give it distinction and charm. One way that this can be done is by using the grey- and silver-foliaged plants that thrive in well-drained, sunny positions, interplanting them with pink flowers, with flowers of pink, mauve and pale blue, or with the bolder scarlet and bronze, or blood crimson and orange combinations.

Pinks and carnations provide both floral and foliage interest with blue-grey leaves and scarlet, yellow, white or crimson flowers. For this reason they are especially useful in such a context. They are particularly at home as edging plants and love the well-drained position provided by a raised bed or border. Both are so well-known that I am pausing here only to suggest two new strains which may easily be raised from seed. Thomson and Morgan now offer seed of a useful strain of carnation, 'Dwarf Chez-nous', the first F_1 hybrid of the genus. Extremely disease-resistant, this strain bears blooms as large as those of a greenhouse carnation on strong rigid stems that do not need support. Hence they are a great boon for the owners of tiny gardens where staking can spoil the natural yet tidy look for which they strive. The plants should be set at least 20 cm (8 in) apart as each attains a spread of 35 cm (14 in). The second strain is a form of the maiden pink. *Dianthus* 'Brilliant' flowers in three months from a spring sowing and forms neat mats of dark foliage, studded with thousands of amaranth-red 'pinks'.

Useful, too, among the silvers are the annual larkspurs, which are daintier in growth than the delphiniums. Their seed can be bought in separate colours of pink, blue or white or in packets of mixed colours. Other members of the supporting cast might include pink, white or flame antirrhinums; pink, scarlet, blood-red or bronze dahlias; pink, white or lavender petunias; and clary (the annual sage), *Salvia horminum*, of which the purple, rose-coloured bracts are the main attraction.

The silver framework can be supplied by such plants as *Stachys lanata*, the old favourite lamb's ears. A non-flowering form of this known as 'Silver Carpet' is obtainable, although I can never understand why people should want this. I think the soft, grey and rose flower spikes are too much a part of the essential charm of the plant to want to dispense with them. The foliage sometimes harbours slugs, so it is essential to remove old leaves and to avoid overcrowding by splitting up the plants every second year.

Senecio cineraria 'White Diamond' is a showy plant with which to keep up the silvery theme. Its flowers are mustard and should be pinched out as soon as shoots emerge, for not only would their colour be devastating to the scheme, but if allowed to grow they would send up a mass of uneven shoots, the removal of which would entail the loss of a great deal of beautiful foliage. So it is necessary to be watchful so as to nip out all flowering shoots as soon as they appear, leaving the silvery rosettes intact.

Artemisias are among the most popular of 'silvers', and with good cause. Compact in growth and with interesting filigree foliage, they add interest and distinction to the border. For this reason they should be planted towards the front and given adequate space so that their beauty will not be cramped or overshadowed. *A. absinthinum* is one of the hardiest, and there is a particularly good form known as 'Lambrook Silver'; this is apt to be expensive because it is difficult to propagate, but it is so good that it is almost indispensable to the 'silver' border. Like all other occupants of such a planting, this artemisia is dual-purpose as its foliage is invaluable for flower arranging. And its tiny yellow bobbles are less destructive to the colour scheme than those of the senecio. However, if one prefers, the blooms can be shared off before they open, and if this is done the bush will remain at about 45 cm (18 in) high and of a similar spread. It has ferny, carroty foliage which emerges pale green and turns to silvery grey. The leaves grow to about 15 cm (6 in) long and almost as much across and last in good condition for several months.

Helichrysums, too, are useful, and *H. fontanesii* from Sicily is one of the most beautiful with feathery, silver foliage. It makes a shrub of 90 cm (3 ft) or more in height by 75 cm (2½ ft) in width and like all 'silvers' is best planted in May when frost danger is past. After that it is usually hardy. The pale yellow flowers can be removed by shearing over the plant as soon as the stems appear. This is beneficial as the flowering stems seem only to sap the vigour of the plant.

Town conditions, as well as being subject to pollution (which many 'silvers' seem able to stand), are apt to prevent many plants from getting sufficient light. Some which seem to survive well enough are *Senecio cineraria* 'White Diamond', *Achillea* 'Moonshine' with pale lemon flower heads, the grey-leaved *Anaphalis triplinervis* with small fluffy white 'Immortelle' blooms, *Artemisia arborescens* and *A. lanata pedemontana*, *Santolina chamaecyparissus*, the lavender cotton, and *Teucrium fruticans* which makes wide silver mats that become smothered with pale lilac bracts in May.

CHAPTER TEN

Shrubs for tiny gardens

Where space is so limited it is even more important than usual to select only the best. Every plant used should be either a personal preference or else chosen for a long period of beauty or double period of interest. Fragrance and evergreen foliage are bonuses. To avoid waste, one should select only those plants that are known to succeed under the particular conditions obtaining in the garden, whether sunny or shady, windy or humid. A list of plants suitable for areas of significant atmospheric pollution will be found at the end of the chapter.

It is important to remember that the tiny garden will have room for only a few shrubs. So it is better to allow those few to develop their full beauty rather than to try to cram in too many. The following list contains only those of suitable size and of real worth. The given size relates to cultivars most suitable for our present purpose. The height is stated before the width.

AUCUBA ($2\frac{1}{2} \times 2$ m (8×6 ft)) Evergreen. The plain green form is recommended for use in areas so heavily polluted that few other evergreens will thrive. Its glossy leaves are handsome and its scarlet winter berries are an added attraction, but both male and female forms must be planted for their production. *A. japonica* 'Nana Rotundifolia' is a useful compact female form.

BERBERIS (90×60 cm (3×2 ft)) (30×45 cm ($1 \times 1\frac{1}{2}$ ft)) Deciduous. Only the purple-foliaged *B. thunbergii atropurpurea* and its cultivar 'Nana' justify space in the tiniest gardens. Their foliage colour contrasts well with the misty blue flowers of caryopteris and perowskia, as well as complementing the silver-kid foliage of *Senecio cineraria* 'White Diamond', the frosted, blue-grey leaves of dianthus and the white flannel of the Jerusalem sage, *Phlomis fruticosa*.

CAMELLIA (2×2 m (6×6 ft)) Evergreen. *C.* $\times$ *williamsii* 'Donation' is the best hybrid of the genus with its profusion of large, double pink flowers. Blooming in early spring, it should be placed against a north- or west-facing wall where the morning sun will not strike the blossoms and so cause ruin after a frosty night. Camellias will not grow well in alkaline soil but in chalky districts they can be grown in tubs or raised beds of lime-free compost. John Innes potting compost No. 3 with flowers of sulphur substituted for chalk may be used, or one may choose the Royal Horticultural Society's recommended compost of 7 parts by bulk of turf loam, 3 of granulated sedge peat, and 2 of gritty, lime-free sand. To each bushel add 42 g (1½ oz) hoof and horn and 42 g (1½ oz) bonemeal. Watering should be carried out only with rain water if the tap water contains lime. Camellias benefit from regular feeding with tea leaves or any form of organic matter which will supply humus, and with special Maxicrop seaweed fertilizer for lime-haters, which contains iron. If yellowing of the foliage should occur due to lime seepage, it can be corrected with Murphy Sequestred Iron at the dose directed on the container. *C. japonica* 'Adolphe Audusson' is a beautiful red which flowers later than 'Donation' and so may be a better choice for cold gardens.

CARYOPTERIS (90 × 90 cm (3 × 3 ft)) Deciduous. *C. clandonensis* is a valuable grey-leaved, aromatic shrub for a raised sunny bed. Its misty blue flower spikes are at their best in August and look very well in association with fuchsias, cistus and lavender. Occasionally it fails to flower, and when this occurs the cause will usually be found to be attack by capsid bugs on the growing tips of the shoots. The remedy is to spray with malathion every three weeks from June until August.

CEANOTHUS (2½ × 2 m (8 × 6 ft)) Evergreen or deciduous (1 × 1 m (4 × 4 ft)). The evergreen hybrids 'Autumnal Blue', 'A. T. Johnson' and 'Burkwoodii' bear their deep blue thimbles of flower in both summer and autumn. They are slightly tender and in the coldest areas should be given a warm wall. The deciduous 'Gloire de Versailles' flowers in August and bears larger panicles of powder blue. It is hardier and so more reliable for cold areas. We find it effective against a wall with rose-red *Hydrangea* 'Vulcan' in front and flanked by the purple-foliaged cotinus. *Ceanothus prostratus* (30 × 90 cm (1 × 3 ft)), evergreen, is a showy blue, mound-forming carpeter which is useful for the front of a border.

CERATOSTIGMA (60 × 90 cm (2 × 3 ft)) Deciduous. *C. willmot-tianum*, the hardy plumbago, carries bright blue flowers in late summer. Not fully hardy, it is best in a raised sunny bed where it may be associated with some of the dwarf shrubby potentillas.

CHAENOMELES (2 × 1 m (6 × 4 ft)) Deciduous. Formerly known as cydonia, it is a member of the same family as the apple, yielding quantities of white to crimson blossom from January to April against a south wall. To give of its best, it should be spur-pruned by cutting back the young shoots to within 1·2 cm ($\frac{1}{2}$ in) of the base in early August. By this means it can be kept small if desired. Among the best varieties are the pink and white 'Apple Blossom', white 'Nivalis', scarlet 'Boule de Feu', 'Knap Hill Scarlet' and the aptly named 'Crimson and Gold'. The double 'Phyllis Moore' is good also and usually flowers very early in winter if grown against a south or west-facing wall.

CHOISYA (2 × 1 m (6 × 4 ft)) Evergreen. *C. ternata* has hand-somely shaped, shiny green leaves and waxy white, scented flowers in May. This, the Mexican orange-blossom, needs a sheltered side in sun or part shade. It is not hardy in cold areas.

CISTUS (60 × 120 cm (2 × 4 ft)) Evergreen. *C. lusitanicus* 'Decumbens' is the only member of the family which is really compact enough for the tiny garden. Its large crinkly sun roses are white with red basal blotches and it flowers from June to September. It is suitable only for a very sunny bed in poor soil and would look well associated with lavender, rosemary and ceratostigma in a raised bed that faces south. For a warm garden the purple to pink *C. creticus* might also be tried or, if particularly appreciated, in suitable settings such as at the seaside, a place might be found for the taller, showy *C. cyprius*.

CORYLOPSIS (1 × 1 m (4 × 4 ft)) Deciduous. Less likely to be spoiled by birds when in blossom in March than the forsythia, *C. pauciflora* is a far better shrub for the tiny garden. Its soft primrose blossoms are airily pretty and its leaves are typical of the hazel family to which it belongs. It will not grow well in very limy soils.

CYTISUS (30 × 90 cm (1 × 3 ft) in the hybrid chosen) Deciduous. Only *C. kewensis*, the dwarf moonlight broom, can really be afforded space in very small gardens, where it will be at its best edging a raised bed so that its well-flowered shoots can make a waterfall of pale sulphur as it cascades over a low wall.

DAPHNE (30–90 × 30–90 cm (1–3 × 1–3 ft)) Evergreen or deciduous. By its fragrance as well as by tradition the February to March-flowering, deciduous, rosy purple *D. mezereum* deserves a place in every garden. There is also a fine creamy white form. The evergreen *D. collina neapolitana* is beautiful with rose-pink, starry flowers against glossy green foliage. This species makes a hummock about 30 cm (1 ft) high and as much across. It has a delightful scent.

ELAEAGNUS (can be kept pruned to 90 × 90 cm (3 × 3 ft)) Evergreen. Only the sunnily variegated *E. pungens* 'Maculata' deserves space in the tiny garden. It can be kept to size by the judicious cutting of sprays of its foliage. Its leaves are entwined with brilliant splashes of daffodil yellow against basic tones of sage and deep bay green. Occasionally the bushes revert to plain green, and any sprays showing this tendency must be cut right out.

EUONYMUS (53 cm (21 in), trailing) Evergreen. The creeping *E. fortunei* 'Variegatus' is worth a place where its ability to cover dry ground in sun or deep shade will be an asset. Its pale green and white leaves become pink-tinged in winter. It resists pollution to some degree.

FATSIA (2 × 1 m (6 × 4 ft)) Evergreen. *F. japonica*, the castor oil plant, is well-known for its handsome foliage and its ability to thrive in the shade of town gardens. It carries large clusters of ivy-like flowers in October and November.

FUCHSIA (90 × 90 cm (3 × 3 ft)) Deciduous. Of the hardy types only the large flowered 'Mrs Popple' and the variegated *F. magellanica* 'Variegata' are worth the precious space a tiny garden can spare. These two are beauties and can be over-wintered successfully in a sunny bed if their crowns are covered with ashes or a 10-cm (4-in) depth of peat. Apart from these, the compact bedding fuchsias are more worthwhile. They can be over-wintered and increased by the methods described in Chapter Four.

GARRYA (2½ × 1 m (8 × 4 ft)) Evergreen. The male form of *G. elliptica* with its long, grey-green tasselled catkins in winter is a fine wall shrub that can be kept pruned so as not to outgrow its space in the very small garden.

HAMAMELIS ($1\frac{1}{2}$ × 1 m (5 × 4 ft)) Deciduous. If your soil is acid or neutral and if winter blossom is important to you, you might find room for *H. mollis* 'Pallida', the showy, pale yellow, ribbon spiders of which last for a full month and look pleasing above a carpet of winter-blooming *Erica carnea* varieties.

HEATHERS (23–60 × 30–60 cm (9–24 × 12–24 in)) Evergreen. From the winter-flowering *Erica carnea* cultivars, through the *E. cinerea*, *E. vagans* kinds and the callunas of summer and autumn, the heaths can be relied on to make neat and floriferous garden furnishings. Some of the most reliable winter-blooming cultivars are *E. carnea* 'Winter Beauty' (rose-purple), 'Vivellii' (red-purple), the white 'Springwood', and its sport 'Springwood Pink'. The 'Springwood' kinds should be set 45 cm (18 in) apart and the others 30 cm (1 ft).

For summer, as far as tiny gardens are concerned, I would discard the *E. cinerea* cultivars and choose these of the showier *E. vagans*, with their long, bottle-brush spikes. The old favourite 'Mrs Maxwell' in deep rose is hard to beat, while the pure white 'Lyonesse' makes a useful contrast.

There are many splendid new cultivars of the autumn-flowering callunas but for our purpose I would choose only three: the golden-foliaged 'Gold Haze' with double white flowers; the rose-pink double, 'H. E. Beale', which is excellent for cutting; and 'Fred J. Chapple', which bears pretty purple flower spikes and has young spring foliage of copper and pink.

HEBE (60 × 60 cm (2 × 2 ft)) Evergreen. These New Zealand shrubs used to be considered hardy only on the coast. However, they will stand most winters in sheltered southern and western gardens. Small gardens by their sheltered nature offer them a good chance of survival, and they are certainly worth a try, especially the *H. × andersonii* varieties with their neat-foliaged, hummocky shapes and lavender-coloured bottle-brush flowers. There is a form with variegated foliage but for some reason I prefer the type.

The violet-purple, bronze-foliaged 'Autumn Glory' is good, as is the compact, pink-flowered 'Great Orme'. Real sun-trap gardens may offer successful homes for the more tender, large-flowered speciosa hybrids with their showier bottle-brushes in crimson and violet.

HIBISCUS (120 × 90 cm (4 × 3 ft)) Deciduous. Hardy hibiscuses need full sun to do well, but if you can give them such a position they are good value in the late summer garden. Three of the most pleasing are 'Blue Bird', the rosy 'Woodbridge' and the white 'Monstrosus'. Their large, hollyhock-type flowers are enlivened by handsome blotches of deep colour.

HYDRANGEA (30–90 × 60–120 cm (1–3 × 2–4 ft)) Deciduous. On limy or neutral soil the flowers will be pink. On acid soil they will be blue. On neutral soil, the blooms may be rendered blue if the plants are treated with commercial alum at the rate of 0·45 kg (1 lb) to each group of five stems, spread over the root area in November and left to be washed in by the rain. The best small-growing hortensia varieties are 'Ami Pasquier' and 'Vulcan'. The only small-growing lacecap forms are 'Seafoam' and 'Whitewave', in both of which the large sterile florets are white. Not fully hardy, in cold areas they should be grown against a wall. The tall *H. paniculata* 'Grandiflora' is hardier and has a different appeal with its plumes of creamy bloom. The laterals of this species should be cut back each year in early spring to within 15 cm (6 in) of the previous year's growth, but the hortensias and lacecaps should have only unwanted wood removed from the base. I leave the dead flower heads on until spring in order to protect the next season's flower-bearing shoots from frost.

HYPERICUM (90 × 120 cm (3 × 4 ft)) Semi-evergreen. 'Hidcote' is the best and hardiest form, bearing large, golden, saucer-shaped flowers from July to October. Sheared over in early spring, it can be kept densely compact. When in flower, it is most effective when associated with blue hydrangeas and the deciduous *Ceanothus* 'Gloire de Versailles'.

LAVANDULA (45 × 45 cm (18 × 18 in)) Evergrey. *L.* 'Hidcote' is the best and most compact form for our purpose. It flowers in July and needs a sunny, well-drained spot. To prevent it becoming straggly it should be clipped back in March, but only the previous season's growth. Older wood should be left uncut.

LUPINUS (90 × 90 cm (3 × 3 ft)) Evergrey. *L. chamissonis* from Hillier's is a valuable silvery-leaved shrublet with misty blue flowers. It needs full sun and well-drained soil and is ideal for a 'grey' or pink and silver border.

MAHONIA (45–150 × 90 cm (1½–5 × 3 ft)) Evergreen. The tall and striking *M. japonica* or the hybrid 'Charity' are shrubs for special placing, with foliage that is beautiful all the year round and scented lemon flower racemes in darkest winter. The lowly *M. aquifolium* is a poor relation but no less useful to beautify a dank basement garden or to survive in dry and dripped-on shade beneath trees.

PAEONIA (120 × 90 cm (4 × 3 ft)) Deciduous. The many lovely hybrid tree or Moutan peonies are valuable spring shrubs of great impact and beauty deserving a place in backyard gardens that are free from May frost. They should be given a stout stake for support.

PERNETTYA (60 × 60 cm (2 × 2 ft)) Evergreen. The Davis's Hybrids of *P. mucronata* are useful berrying shrubs to associate with heaths in a restricted bed where their suckers cannot wander too far. Their berries, like coloured marbles, range from white through pink and crimson to mulberry and last all winter. They will not do well on chalky soil.

PEROWSKIA (90 × 60 cm (3 × 2 ft)) Deciduous. A misty blue and silver shrublet for a sunny, raised bed. Charming with lavender, *Lupinus chamissonis* and sedums.

PHILADELPHUS (90 × 90 cm (3 × 3 ft)) Deciduous. The best mock oranges for our purpose are those of the smallest growth. The double 'Albâtre' is rigidly narrow and very fragrant. 'Avalanche' is semi-erect in growth and charming with a profusion of snowy, single flowers which weigh down the branches. 'Manteau d'Hermine' and *P. microphyllus* are also suitable, as is the purple-centred 'Bicolore'. Perhaps Hillier's of Winchester have the widest selection.

PHLOMIS (60 × 60 cm (2 × 2 ft)) Evergrey. *P.* 'Edward Bowles' is the most suitable Jerusalem sage for the tiny garden. Sub-shrubby, it has large, frosted grey, heart-shaped leaves and sulphur-yellow flower croziers. It needs a dryish, sunny spot.

PIERIS (90 × 60 cm (3 × 2 ft)) Evergreen. *P. taiwanensis* 'Crispa' is the only one that is really small enough for our selection. It is most attractive with coppery young growths and waterfalls of lily-of-the-valley flowers. As the cultivar name indicates, the margin of the leaves are wavy. Like all members of the *Ericaceae*, it must have an acid or neutral soil.

POTENTILLA (45 × 60 cm (1½ × 2 ft)) Deciduous. An extremely useful and attractive genus which has some pleasing dwarfs. They will thrive in sun or semi-shade and their flowers, which are like small, single roses, are displayed from June until November. Should they show signs of becoming straggly, they should be well cut back after flowering. Good for the tiny garden are *P. arbuscula* 'Beesii', with silver foliage and golden flowers, and 'Farmer's White', also 'Gold Drop' and 'Tangerine', the names of which relate to their flower colour.

PUNICA (45 × 60 cm (1½ × 2 ft)) Evergreen. *P. granatum* 'Nana', the dwarf pomegranate, is a charming shrub for a sunny wall and well-drained soil. Its funnel-shaped orange-scarlet flowers appear in September and October.

PYRACANTHA (1–1½ × 1½ m (3–5 × 5 ft)) Deciduous. Wall shrubs which respond well to pruning. The hawthorn-like flowers are pleasant in May but the chief glory is in the berries. Two to resist the birds are the yellow-fruited 'Buttercup' and the new American hybrid 'Shawnee', which can be obtained from Hillier's. Its orange-yellow berries colour from August onwards.

RHODODENDRON (including the azalea series) (Those reaching a size of only 60 × 60 cm (2 × 2 ft) are most suitable for the purpose of the dwarf shrub or heather bed) Evergreen. Dwarf, tiny-leaved rhododendron species and hybrids, together with the evergreen azaleas, are the ones that concern us here. Some of the best for the tiny garden are the 'Forrest's Dwarf' form of the early-flowering *R. racemosum*, the slightly later, soft blue *R. lapponicum* and the brighter blue *R. scintillans*. *R. hanceanum* 'Nanum' is an attractive, soft-yellow-flowered dwarf and there is also the interesting *R. campylogynum myrtilloides* with rosy thimble flowers. Slightly later to bloom is the raspberry-red alpen rose, *R. ferrugineum*. Together with the hybrid 'Pink Drift', the spreading scarlet 'Jenny' and the evergreen azaleas in pink, white, mauve, crimson and scarlet, they offer exciting planting prospects for acid soil. Rhododendron enthusiasts might make room also for the columnar 'Yellow Hammer', the slow-growing blood-red 'Humming Bird', the early lavender 'Praecox', and 'Lady Chamberlain' with its drooping salmon and yellow bells.

ROBINIA (2 × 1 m (6 × 3 ft)) Deciduous. *R. kelseyi* of the brittle branches and lilac-rose pea-type flowers will justify a sheltered place. Flowering in June, its foliage, too, is elegant.

ROSE (90 × 90 cm (3 × 3 ft)) Deciduous. The best value among roses for tiny gardens is probably to be found in the floribunda section where small-growing varieties such as 'Allgold', the two-toned pink 'Dearest', velvety crimson 'Lilli Marlene', and apricot 'Woburn Abbey' are among the best. Watch also for such compact new varieties as 'Meteor' (orange-scarlet), 'Tip-Top' (salmon), 'Kerry Gold', 'Snowline' (white) and 'Sunday Times' (cherry pink). All these will flower freely over a very long period. Hybrid tea enthusiasts, of course, will want to include one or two of their own favourites. Climbing varieties, also, may be used on walls.

SALIX (30 × 60 cm (1 × 2 ft)) Deciduous. *S. repens* and its variety *S. argentea* will provide the catkin lover with delightful silver 'pussy' catkins in spring. Normally a creeping shrub, this dwarf willow can easily be controlled within the confines of a small, raised bed.

SKIMMIA (60 × 60 cm (2 × 2 ft)) Evergreen. Most valuable for gardens on acid soil is the hermaphroditic dwarf *S. reevesiana*, but for limy soils, in order to obtain berries, it will be necessary to plant both the compact female *S. japonica* 'Rogersii' and its male counterpart, the even smaller *S. j.* 'Rogersii Nana', the red buds of which are pleasing throughout the winter. For the tiny garden, skimmias make decorative evergreen furnishings. Not only are they smaller than holly – and without prickles – but they are more reliable in berry.

SPIRAEA (120 × 90 cm (4 × 3 ft)) Deciduous. *S. thunbergii* is smaller and of denser growth than the better known *S. arguta* (foam of May). It flowers even earlier in March, and blooms throughout April, the branches becoming crowded with its decorative pure white blossom. *S. japonica* flowers later, from midsummer on, and offers two good dwarf forms which make compact little bushes that cover themselves with rose-red flowers. They are *S. j.* 'Alpina', which is suitable even for a window-box, and *S. j.* 'Bullata'. Also good is the slightly larger-growing, bright crimson *S. × bumalda* 'Anthony Waterer'.

SYRINGA (lilac) (120 × 90 cm (4 × 3 ft)) Deciduous. *S. × persica* 'Alba' is the form that best justifies a place in the tiny garden as it is sufficiently like the larger hybrids in appearance to gratify the desire to grow a lilac of one's own. Not so identifiable in flower is the nonetheless sweetly scented *S. microphylla* 'Superba', the blossom of which is rosy pink in colour.

VIBURNUM (90–120 × 90 cm (3–4 × 3 ft)) Deciduous in selected forms. The winter-flowering *V. farreri* (syn. *V. fragrans*) and its hybrid *V.* × *bodnantense* are too strong-growing for most tiny gardens. *V. foetens* is a relative of smaller growth which opens its sweetly scented white flowers from pale pink buds from January on. It appreciates a moist position in semi-shade.

Of the spring-flowering viburnums, we find the hybrid *V.* × *juddii* the most reliable, being less subject to die-back and aphis attack than the original *V. carlesii*. In flower the two are very much alike with sweetly scented, rose-tinged, bun heads of milky white flowerlets.

Of the summer-blooming members of the family, choice for the smaller garden is difficult, owing to their vigour. From the beautiful lacecaps, which cover their horizontal tiers in May and June with a magnificent foam of blossom, I would select 'Rowallane', as this is rather less strong-growing than its near relatives. It is, in any case, not too difficult to control the spread by cutting the flower-laden branches to decorate the house. In our garden we have a nine-year-old bush which we have successfully kept by this means to a height of 75 cm (2½ ft) with a 90-cm (3-ft) spread. To my mind the more familiar snowball types of viburnum are too strong-growing and not sufficiently distinguished for the tiny garden, with the possible exception of *V. plicatum* itself, the Japanese snowball, which used to be known as *V. tomentosum* 'Sterile'.

WEIGELA (1½ × 1 m (5 × 4 ft)) Deciduous. Only two, the dual-purpose June-flowering, *W. florida* 'Variegata', with its green and cream leaves and pink summer flowers, and *W. middendorffiana*, with its peeling bark and sulphur-yellow, foxglove flowers in April, really earn their space in the tiny garden. They should be pruned only by cutting out unwanted wood from the base.

Note. Of the genera mentioned in this chapter, the most resistant to atmospheric pollution are: aucuba, berberis, camellia, ceanothus (deciduous types), ceratostigma, chaenomeles, cistus, cytisus, daphne, elaeagnus, fatsia, garrya, hibiscus, hydrangea, hypericum, mahonia, pernettya, philadelphus, pyracantha, rosa, skimmia, spiraea, syringa, viburnum and weigela.

CHAPTER ELEVEN

Some worthwhile perennials

In the tiny garden there is no room for plants that do not pull their weight. Only those with a reliably long season of flowering can be considered.

In such close confines staking is 'out'. So we are looking for self-supporting plants of firm and moderate growth. Handsome foliage or scent when they occur are a *plus*.

In the following list, the figures in brackets refer to the size of an established clump. The height is given first.

ACHILLEA (60 × 30 cm (2 × 1 ft)). *A.* 'Moonshine', with its lemon-yellow, plate-like heads of flowers, is one of the best for the tiny garden. In flower June–August.

ALCHEMILLA (45 × 45 cm (18 × 18 in)). *A. mollis* is worth growing for its beautifully lobed and felted apple-green leaves as well as for its froth of greeny yellow flowers. June–August.

ANEMONE (45 × 30 cm (18 × 12 in)). The single white 'Louise Uhink' and the slightly taller, pink 'September Charm' kinds of *A.* × *hybrida* (syn. *A. japonica*) should be planted in spring. They prefer a moist, semi-shady position and are valuable additions to the autumn garden. September–October.

AQUILEGIA (columbine) (60–90 × 15 cm (2–3 ft × 6 in)). These elegant, airy and prettily coloured flowers are easily grown from seed but can also be bought as established plants. They enjoy a rich soil and will grow in semi-shade. May–June.

ASTILBE (60 × 45 cm (2 × 1½ ft)). Dark red 'Fanal', pink 'Rhineland' and white 'Gloria' are three of the smaller-growing, herbaceous spiraeas. They look well by a pool but will grow in any rich, moist soil and enjoy shade. June–August.

BERGENIA (30 × 30 cm (1 × 1 ft)). The rose-pink *B. cordifolia* produces its fleshy pink flower spikes in early spring but it is also grown for its handsome leaves. If planted in full sun and poor soil, the foliage will redden attractively in winter. The white 'Silver Light' and purple-crimson 'Evening Glow' are worth growing in addition to the species.

CAMPANULA. *C. persicifolia* (90 × 30 cm (3 × 1 ft)) is the best of the taller sorts for the tiny garden. 'Telham Beauty' in harebell blue and the double white 'Fleur de Neige' are the varieties to pick, flowering June–August. *C.* 'Pouffe' makes a 30 cm (1 ft) high mound for the front of the border and is very pretty with its silver-blue flowers.

CATANANCHE (Cupid's dart) (60 × 30 cm (2 × 1 ft)). *C. caerulea* is an attractive perennial cornflower with lavender-blue flowers that can be dried for winter use. June–September.

CHRYSANTHEMUM. The double white 'Esther Read' really takes up too much space for the tiny garden, but *C. rubellum* 'Clara Curtis' (75 × 30 cm (2½ × 1 ft)) is a pink-flowered chrysanthemum that is useful in autumn.

COREOPSIS (60 × 45 cm (2 × 1½ ft)). *C. auriculata* 'Superba', with gay yellow daisy flowers, zoned with crimson, is the best for the tiny garden. It is good enough to earn a sunny space. June–September.

DELPHINIUM. The shorter varieties such as 'Blue Tit', 'Blue Jade' and 'Betty Bazely', together with the loosely spiked *belladonna* forms, are best for the tiny garden. They grow to about 120 cm (4 ft) high by about 30 cm (1 ft) across. They should not need staking in an enclosed garden. Slugs are their main enemy, and these can be kept at bay by scraping away the top 2½ cm (1 in) of soil and covering the crowns with sharp horticultural sand. Delphiniums need a rich, well-dug soil. June–July.

DIANTHUS (23 × 45 cm (9 × 18 in)). The various strains of *allwoodii* dianthus and border pinks are ideal for small, sunny gardens. Raised beds suit them well. They do not need too rich a soil and even when out of flower are attractive with their blue-grey foliage. 'Swanlake', 'Doris', 'Joan', 'Enchantress', and 'Cherry Ripe' are all good varieties, and also the old but completely reliable and strongly scented 'Sinkins'. June–September.

DICENTRA (bleeding heart) (60 × 45 cm (2 × 1½ ft.)) *D. spectabilis* is a showy plant for early summer with attractive ferny foliage and conspicuous rose and white heart-shaped lockets. It does well in semi-shade and needs only a mulch of rotted compost each spring. Slugs are its worst enemy. May–June.

DICTAMNUS (60 × 30 cm (2 × 1 ft)). Both the rosy red *D. purpureus* and the white *D. albus* are good forms of the burning bush. The white is perhaps the most beautiful but both are deserving of space. June–July.

DIERAMA (60 × 75 cm (2 × 2½ ft)). The wand flowers are beautiful plants, and the dwarf form of *D. pulcherrimum* is especially suitable for a small garden. In a raised bed they can be associated with heliotrope and fuchsias, or towards the front of a border they can sway above the dwarf erigerons and sedums. September–October.

DIMORPHOTHECA (30 × 75 cm (1 × 2½ ft)). *D. barberiae*, a pretty pink daisy from the Cape, makes dense mats of foliage above which rise the attractive lilac-rose flowers. It is generally hardy, at any rate in the south and west, but should have a sunny spot in well-drained soil. A raised bed is ideal. May–October.

ERIGERON. Most of the present-day hybrids grow to about 60 cm (2 ft) tall and make mats about 45 cm (1½ ft) across. They may need the support of twiggy sticks to prevent them from flopping. 'Charity', 'Felicity' and 'Serenity' are all good in various shades of mauve. June–August.

EUPHORBIA (23 × 30 cm (9 × 12 in)). *E. epithymoides* is a beautiful low-growing subject for early spring with sea-green fleshy foliage and sharp yellow bracts. March–April.

GERANIUM (45 × 45 cm (18 × 18 in)). *G. endressii* 'A. T. Johnson' and *G. grandiflorum* 'Johnson's Blue' are the best for our purpose. They will thrive in any soil in sun or semi-shade. *G. endressii* flowers from June to October but *G. grandiflorum* flowers only in June and July. It is so pretty, though, as to be worth a place if room can be found. With its densely attractive foliage it makes fine ground cover.

HEUCHERA (45 × 30 cm (18 × 12 in)). The Bressingham Hybrids are the best forms of this superior London pride-type of plant. The leaves are more elegant than those of its plebeian relation and the red and pink flower plumes are distinctive and showy. Light and airy and taking up little room, the heucheras are worth planting in even the smallest space. July–August.

HOSTA. Beloved of the flower arranger and useful for foliage emphasis. The variegated *H. undulata* and *H. fortunei* 'Albotpicta' are the two most worth a place in limited space. They need moist, rich soil and make sizeable clumps of 60–75 cm (2–2½ ft) across. The lily-like mauve flowers open July–August.

IRIS (45 × 45–60 cm (1½ × 1½–2 ft)). Only the more dwarf forms can really be spared room in the tiny garden and these must have full sun and good drainage. 'Green Spot' is one of the best, while 'Gold Fan' and 'Blue Denim' are also good. May–June.

LIATRIS (90 × 45 cm (3 × 1½ ft)). *L. spicata* is a showy border plant with a red-hot poker type of truncheon-like spike in purple. It does best in full sun and a light soil. July–August.

LUPIN (90 × 60 cm (3 × 2 ft)). The tiny garden may have room for only one clump in its border but even so it will be worth having, flowering as it will in June before many of the other border flowers are out.

MECONOPSIS (75 × 30 cm (2½ × 1 ft)). The blue poppy, *M. betonicifolia* is a wonderful plant, with nodding, saucer-shaped flowers of kingfisher-blue. It needs the special care the keen owner of a tiny garden is sometimes prepared to give. Moist, acid soil and partial shade are *musts*. Also seedlings should never be allowed to flower in their first year or they may die. This entails pinching out the flower stems as they develop in the first summer, after which they will go on to form strong perennial clumps. June–July.

MONARDA (90 × 45 cm (3 × 1½ ft)). The bergamot has striking whorls of curiously attractive flowers, crowning and circling the stems, and held high above the aromatic leaves. 'Croftway Pink' and 'Cambridge Scarlet' are two of the best varieties. They need moisture if they are not to die out. June–September.

NEPETA (catmint) (30 × 60 cm (1 × 2 ft)). The smaller-growing *N. faassenii* is the most suitable plant for a tiny garden where it might be used to top a sunny retaining wall. May–September.

PAEONIA (90 × 45 cm (3 × 1½ ft)). The July-flowering *P. lactiflora* types are the best value for the little garden. They are so beautiful that they cannot be ignored but they often need staking. To get the best from them, beware of planting the tubers too deep: 5 cm (2 in) below the soil surface is enough. They appreciate a generous helping of rotted compost or manure dug deeply into the soil. Their roots should never actually come into contact with the manure. The old cottage garden *P. officinalis* might also find a home. A clump of the double crimson type can be very showy in May.

PHYSOSTEGIA (obedient plant) (60 × 30 cm (2 × 1 ft)). *P. virginiana* 'Vivid' is useful on account of its flowering time, its bright rose flower spikes remaining colourful from August until frost. It will grow in sun or shade. There is also a white variety.

PLATYCODON (45 × 45 cm (18 × 18 in)). *P. grandiflorus* mariesii is a wonderful front row plant for a sunny border with its bright blue, balloon-shaped bells. July–September.

POLYGONATUM (Solomon's seal) (75 × 60 cm (2½ × 2 ft)). *P. multiflorum* is useful for shady sites and attractive with its arching stems of pendant ivory bells. May–June.

PRIMULA. The Asiatic primulas such as the crimson *P. japonica*, tall, yellow, sweetly scented *P. sikkimensis* and rose-pink 'Bartley Strain' of *P. pulverulenta* are beautiful speciality plants for rich, good, moist soil in semi-shade. Flowering from April until July they reach 45–60 cm (1½–2 ft) tall. They are easily raised from seed, of which Thompson and Morgan, of London Road, Ipswich, supply a good mixture. We find the seeds germinate best if sown in a peaty mixture topped with chippings, in a box or an alpine pan, and stood outside under a north-facing wall in February. When four of the young leaves show in April, they should be transferred to a nursery corner and grown on in peaty soil. In the autumn they will be ready to be moved to their permanent positions to flower the following spring. The early drumstick *P. denticulata*, whether with white or lavender flowers, is good also.

PYRETHRUM. P. 'Eileen May Robinson' (pink) and 'Kelway's Glorious' (crimson) are two of the best of these ferny-foliaged daisies. They grow to about 60 cm (2 ft) in height and make clumps about 30 cm (1 ft) across. They are easily grown in sun or shade. If the flowered stems are cut down when the blooms fade they will usually bloom again. May–June and September.

RUDBECKIA. The new, seed-raised Tetra Gloriosa hybrids that can be bought with the bedding plants in spring are best and will often go on to become reliable perennials. Plant three to a 60 cm (2 ft) square. Flowers from August to frost.

SALVIA (45 × 30 cm (18 × 12 in)). *S. superba* 'Lubeca' is a showy sage. Its deep blue flowers in early summer are followed by attractive purple bracts. It is a good plant for a sunny border.

SCABIOUS (75 × 30 cm (2½ × 1 ft)). The old lavender-blue favourite, S. 'Clive Greaves' has companions in the frilly, pinkish 'Loddon Anna' and the lovely 'Loddon White'. Easy to grow, they prefer sun and are best planted in spring. June–September.

SCHIZOSTYLIS (45 × 15 cm (18 × 6 in)). Scarlet *S. coccinea* and pale pink 'Viscountess Byng' are useful and easy rhizomatous subjects. Like tiny gladioli, the type flowers from September to November. 'Viscountess Byng' flowers from October on and so needs a sunny, sheltered, spot. Protect with peat in cold areas during severe weather.

SEDUM (45 × 45 cm (18 × 18 in)). The ice plant *S. spectabile* with its fleshy pale leaves and mauve-pink flat heads of flowers, is neat and colourful from August to October. Even better are the slightly taller *S. maximum* 'Atropurpureum', with dark-toned stems and leaves, and the brighter pink 'Brilliant'. They are all useful in attracting the butterflies and for this purpose are much more satisfactorily and easily accommodated in the little garden than the buddleias with their leggy growth and too quickly browning flower plumes. Sedums need some sun but they are drought-resistant and very hardy. August-November.

STACHYS (45 × 90 cm (1½ × 3 ft)). *S. lanata*, lamb's ears, is one of my favourite plants. The tiny garden may have room for only one clump of its silky grey foliage and pleasantly muted grey and pink flower spikes, but it certainly *should* be included. Happy in sun or semi-shade, it is a fine plant for the front of a border or to edge a rose bed or path. Flowering mainly in July and August, the appeal of its foliage is nevertheless all the year round.

THALICTRUM (120 × 45 cm (4 × 1½ ft)). *T. aquilegifolium* grows tall but it takes up little space and its cloud of tiny, soft purple flowers is so pretty that it should be given a place. It does best in well-drained yet rich, moist soil, and to achieve this should be top-dressed with moist peat in May. The dwarf form 'Purple Cloud' (75 × 45 cm (2½ × 1½ ft)) should be planted whenever available. May–July.

TRADESCANTIA (30 × 30 cm (1 × 1 ft)). The pale blue 'J. C. Weguelin' and white 'Osprey' are pretty unusual with their three-petalled flowers. They typify the uncommon, characterful and showy plants for which space should be found in even the tiniest gardens. June–September.

VERONICA (45 × 45 cm (18 × 18 in)). *V. spicata* in its blue and pink-flowered varieties is so neat and attractive as to be easily accommodated. It prefers sun but will flower quite well in partial shade. June–August.

Herbaceous plants which will stand heavy atmospheric pollution include:

Anemone × *hybrida* varieties	Erigeron
Aquilegia	Heuchera
Bergenia	Iris
Coreopsis	Tradescantia
Dicentra	

CHAPTER TWELVE

Bulbs take up little space

Bulbous subjects deserve a special place in the affections of the owners of tiny gardens because not only are they beautiful but, almost without exception, they take up so little room. They can be tucked into odd corners to add interest and charm.

A tiny garden seems to me a wonderful place in which to indulge in the growing of special treasures, because in so small an area it is easy to keep them all under one's eye. And of all the candidates for cherishment, of course, the small bulbs and corms are the most appropriate, just because they do take up so little space.

In many people's minds, the word 'bulb' is associated mainly with spring. Yet, to the enthusiast, the bulb year may well start in July with the planting of the autumn crocuses. These lovely little plants, which are not technically 'bulbs' but corms, can often be bought comparatively cheaply and should be planted in drifts of two dozen or more bulbs. Less would not make a noticeable display. To my mind one of the great things when planting small bulbs is to plant them in natural-looking clumps or 'drifts' wherever possible so that they look as if they had sprung up naturally. The autumn crocus is too delicately lovely a flower to be regimented into lines and squares. There are two kinds of plant loosely referred to as 'autumn crocus'. One is the true autumn crocus, of which the species *zonatus* and *speciosus* are the ones to choose for cheapness and reliability. The others are the colchicums which make much untidy 'grass' (leaves) in spring and so are unsuitable for the tiny garden.

The main difference between a bulb and a corm is that a bulb lives on from year to year, increasing by splitting to form new bulbs. A corm (crocus and gladiolus for instance) dies after flowering, and an entirely new corm and offsets are formed below it. This shows how important it is not to disturb a patch of corms until its cycle of development is completed. Otherwise you may lose the new corms, and so your whole stock of the flowers.

Many people are tempted to remove the dying leaves of bulbs. This is a bad practice and will result in the non-flowering and eventual death of the bulbs. Bulbs and corms not only contain the embryo of the complete flower and leaves, but they are also storehouses of food, often holding all the nourishment the plant will need during its cycle of growth and flowering. Bulbs draw nourishment from the soil through their roots. This is sent up to the leaves, which are at the same time drawing food from the air. This food is stored in the leaves while the bulb is growing. As the flower and leaves die, the nourishment is drawn back into the bulb. It is wise always to remove the faded flowerhead, so that the bulb does not exhaust itself by setting seed. However, it is vital to leave the foliage, and, if possible, the flower stalk, to feed the bulb until they wither. For this reason daffodils and other bulbs used for bedding out should not be lifted immediately after flowering unless strictly necessary.

Several charming, bulbous plants flower in autumn in addition to the crocus. For a sunny border there are the zephyranthes, or flowers of the west wind, lovely starry blooms in white or rose-pink of which the white is the hardier and more reliable. Even so it is often quite difficult to establish. Like a much bigger crocus and golden in colour are the sturdy sternbergias, sometimes said to be the lilies of the field mentioned in the Bible. These also appreciate a well-drained, sunny spot.

To my mind, the queen of the autumn bulbous flowers is the nerine, which is hardy in sunny, sheltered positions – particularly under a south or south-west wall. The nerine has beautiful pink flowers, similar in shape to those of an amaryllis, but with much-divided petals, giving a lighter, feathery appearance. *Nerine bowdenii* is the species to plant. It flowers in September and October while the spring-flowering bulbs are still being got into the ground.

When considering daffodils for the tiny garden it is wisest to discard the bigger-flowered varieties which have large leaves to match and which can present a problem as the foliage dies. No true gardener, though, would be without daffodils at spring time, so when dealing with limited space it becomes a matter of choosing either the *Narcissus triandrus* or the *N. cyclamineus* hybrids which make smaller growth and have narrower and shorter 'grass', which is not as unsightly while withering as that of the larger varieties. Even so, it is a good idea to plant the daffodils among July–August-flowering herbaceous plants, the foliage of which will be low when the narcissi are in flower but which will quickly grow to hide the dying leaves of the bulbs when the blooms are over.

The narcissus season starts with tiny species for the rock garden like *N. cyclamineus*, with its fly-away perianth and long narrow golden trumpet. This little daffodil grows well in a moist, rather acid spot, where it can be followed by the hoop petticoat, *N. bulbocodium* with its yellow, crinoline frill.

Rather larger are the early hybrids, which can be accommodated in the flower beds, at the forefront of shrubs, or in window-boxes or tubs. One of the best of these is 'February Gold', which is shortly followed by 'Peeping Tom' with an extra-long golden trumpet. The more lightly built 'March Sunshine' flowers next, along with the pale-coloured 'W. P. Milner' and 'Rosy Trumpet'. Later come such triandrus hybrids as 'April Tears' and 'Liberty Bells', which bear several elegantly drooping flowers in white or yellow on a stem.

Snowdrops, unfortunately, do not always succeed at first planting. They should, if possible, be bought 'in the green' and planted as the flowers die down in spring. Failing this, set the bulbs in a temporary position in early autumn, then dig them up and move them to their permanent site as the flowers fade in March. This usually has the effect of making them settle down and become permanent inhabitants of the garden.

For some reason, we have never been able to get the green-ruffed winter aconites (*Eranthis*) to succeed permanently in our own garden; yet, where it is happy, the common *E. hyemalis* can become almost a weed. The bronze-foliaged *E.* × *tubergenii* bears larger flowers of deeper gold and so is better garden value where only a few can be grown.

Some people regard the common grape hyacinth (muscari) as a nuisance with its prolific foliage, but its bright blue closely packed thimbles of bells are beautiful and I like to see it at the base of a tree, or edging a path or window-box in front of a band of yellow poly-anthus primulas. It is pretty, too, in association with the ubiquitous magenta *Primula* 'Wanda'. In fact the juxtaposition seems to bring out the best of both of these sometimes maligned plants. In addition to *Muscari* 'Heavenly Blue', the Cambridge blue *M. armeniacum* 'Cantab' and white *M. botryoides album* are well worth growing.

Scillas, both the brilliant *S. sibirica* and *S. bifolia*, should always be planted, together with the starry blue and white chionodoxas and the paler puschkinias. One cannot have too many different sorts of these easy and attractive little bulbs.

Another beauty for a special position is the snowflake, *Leucojum vernum*, which flowers rather later than the common snowdrop but is about the same size, though with rather more substance. Its hanging bells are like tiny lampshades and the petal points are tipped with green or yellow. A planting of half a dozen bulbs in well-drained soil in sun or semi-shade will increase to a sizeable clump.

Among the loveliest of the bulbous plants are the various species of hardy cyclamen, all of which require a well-drained loamy soil. They will be happy on a rock garden, in a pocket of good soil among the roots of trees, or at the forefront of a border of small shrubs. It is important to choose a site where they will not be overgrown by other plants.

The species most commonly seen are the winter-flowering *C. orbiculatum* (which now includes *C. coum*) and the autumn-blooming *C. neapolitanum*. Both species are delightful. *C. orbiculatum* has dark green rounded leaves and rounded shuttlecock flowers of white, pink or crimson, which associate well with early snowdrops such as the giant *Galanthus elwesii*, with *Iris histrioides*, and with winter aconites, all of which do well in a sunny place. The autumn-flowering *Cyclamen neapolitanum* has heart-shaped leaves beautifully marked with silver and longer-petalled, more elegant, shuttlecock blooms in white or pink. We also grow the spring-flowering *C. repandum*, which we find needs a sunny, well-drained spot and does well in a crevice where moisture drains more easily from its crown, and the scented *C. europaeum*, which flowers in July and does well in semi-shade.

Also delightful are the spring-flowering dog's tooth violets, the erythroniums, with their airy turncap flowers. With these, leaf-mould and a place in the sun, or dappled shade, will result in ever-increasing returns. One can plant *Erythronium dens-canis* in its various colour forms for early bloom with the taller, more elegant *E. californicum* 'White Beauty' to follow. All have handsome, marbled leaves.

So much for a few of the lesser-known bulbous subjects that can be used to enliven tiny gardens. Now for the big drums of spring, the hyacinths, the tulips in their many varieties, and the fat Dutch crocuses which, with the even earlier 'rock garden crocuses' like the amethyst *C. tomasinianus* and the blue, white, yellow and striped *chrysanthus* varieties, bring out the true gaiety of the season.

As I mentioned in an earlier chapter, crocuses in town gardens seem to suffer less than those grown in the country from depradations by mice and voles. Even so, it is worth taking precautions to discourage these predators, either by wrapping the bulbs in flattened 'parcels' of close mesh chicken wire or by surrounding each planting with a palisade of prickly shoots such as those of holly, gorse or berberis.

Hyacinths always look more at home in tiny formal plots than they do in larger country gardens. They are ideal subjects for window-boxes, troughs or tubs, or they can be planted towards the front of beds or borders. A raised bed around the bole of a tree would make a most attractive setting for them also, but wherever you decide to grow them, be sure to plant them in groups of one variety or, if you are contemplating a mixed planting, be sure to select varieties which flower at the same time. The flowering of the following varieties should coincide:

Early	'Anne Marie' (bright pink)
	'Perle Brillante' (pale blue)
	'Ostara' (dark blue)
Mid-season	'L'Innocence' (white)
	'Lady Derby' (light salmon-pink)
	'Jan Bos' (red)
	'Myosotis' (light blue)
Late	'Edelweiss' (white)
	'Winston Churchill' (sky-blue)
	'King of the Blues' (dark blue)

Larger daffodils for window-boxes and troughs might include such well-tried and less expensive varieties as the yellow 'Carlton', 'John Evelyn', with its frilly apricot cup, and the scarlet and gold 'Rustom Pasha'.

The so-called 'Rock garden tulips' may not always succeed as permanent inhabitants in town gardens, although in some places where they can be offered sunny positions in deep but well-drained soil they may form clumps. Hybrids vary from the lowly and colourful varieties of the water lily tulip, *T. kaufmanniana*, in shades of scarlet and cream, yellow and terracotta, to the blood-red or primrose *greigii* hybrids with their handsomely mottled foliage and the taller, brilliant fosterianas with flowers which open flat to as much as 25 cm (10 in) across, showing black centres zoned with a striking yellow band. Named varieties include the scarlet 'Princeps', fiery 'Madame Lefeber', cream and carmine 'Cherry Flip' and the yellow and red 'Easter Parade'.

The 'Dutch' florists' tulips vary in height and times of flowering to give a variety of uses and to cover a long season. Best and longest-lasting for window-boxes and tubs are the dwarf doubles. For bedding one can choose from the single earlies, the mid-season cottage types with their more subtle colours, the striped Rembrandts, the exotic Parrots, the stately Darwins in their many colour forms, the artistically shaped lily-flowered varieties and the peony-flowered late doubles. To them must now be added the multifloras which bear several flowers on a single stem and so make considerable impact in the border.

The cycle of the bulbous irises starts with the bright blue *I. histrioides major*, the brilliant little flowers of which pierce the January snows to make pools of beauty with *Cyclamen orbiculatum* and winter aconite. This species is followed in February by the violet-scented *I. reticulata* and its various forms and hybrids, of which 'Joyce' is perhaps the most showy and generally satisfactory. In May come the Dutch irises, in blue, white, gold and bronze, to be followed closely by the Spanish varieties of similar colouring. And later come the English irises with their more rounded petals and blooms of greater substance. Varieties in white, purple, claret and blue can be bought. They need rather more moisture than the Dutch irises, and a richer soil, but when they are well suited they will go on and increase for years. We have had a clump of one of the white varieties for more than eleven years. It was started by a few bulbs from the garden of a friend who had brought them from her mother's garden twenty years previously.

Some people find difficulty in growing the De Caen and St Brigid anemones with their brilliantly assorted blossoms. These are easy, however, provided the dried corms are soaked in water for twenty-four hours before planting. The same principle applies to the too seldom seen 'Turban' ranunculus (which should be planted in February). The French anemones enjoy a sunny spot where they will reward November planting with early blooms. For shady positions the blue, daisy-petalled *Anemone appenina* is more sure of success. This increases well to make shining pools of blue in May. Some gardeners find the earlier *A. blanda* from Greece, in its various forms of pink and blue, to be more reliable. In some gardens it spreads to make wide carpets beneath the winter-bare branches of deciduous trees. For some reason this species has never stayed for long with us in our North Wales garden. It may be a question of climate. Possibly *A. blanda* does better in the drier, sunnier south. Certainly, in North Wales *A. appenina* is the species more generally seen as a successful carpeter.

The large-flowered gladioli are not favourites of ours, and I think many people might find them a little overpowering within the confines of a tiny garden – though there may be a place for them in an island bed of mixed flowers where they can spear through the foliage of the herbaceous subjects. In this case they should be planted in circular groups of six, perhaps to surround a lupin or other earlier-flowering plant. Such placing will help to avoid the spotty effect that might result were they dotted throughout the border.

Babianas, ixias, watsonias, tigridias and other miscellaneous subjects can be tried if you can spare a sunny spot and have moist, well-drained soil. Certainly the babianas and watsonias are lovely and worthwhile. We find that ixias soon die out, but of a clump of six assorted tigridias we planted seven years ago one pink-flowered bulb survived and has now increased to form a clump of nine. Provided we do not disturb them, I expect they will be with us for years, increasing all the time. This is an instance where a climatically borderline bulb has found the one spot in the garden that suits it and settled down to become at home.

Alliums, the ornamental onions, have in their genus one or two treasures that are well worth garden space. They are particularly valuable as most of them flower in summer. Some species such as the golden *A. moly* and white *A. triquetrum* are to be avoided as they spread too quickly; but the blue stars of *A. beesianum* make this worth a place in good, moist soil. Most of the others prefer a dry spot in the sun, especially the large-headed *A. albopilosum* (lilac), *A. caeruleum* (deep blue) and *A. giganteum* (violet). Flower arrangers will find the alliums more useable if they immerse the stems in tepid water overnight before arranging them next day, to give them a chance to lose their oniony smell.

Lilies are apt to be expensive, but often in the tiny garden one feels the space to be gardened is so small that one can afford this kind of luxury. For a sunny, fairly open border, the madonna lily, *Lilium candidum*, of cottage gardens, is hard to beat. It should be planted at the end of July or in August while in growth. Other lilies are best planted in October, or, failing this, in February, but we have always had the best results from October-planted bulbs.

If you like white lilies, the July-flowering *L. regale* is easy and attractive. Its large white trumpets are stained on the outside with purple and it has a pleasantly opulent scent. Some people dislike white lilies though, so if you are among them, or if you are looking for colour, you cannot do better than try some of the ultra-hardy and exceptionally easy lilies introduced from North America by the Cheshire Bulb Farms, and increased by them in this country (10 Maynestone Road, Chinley, Cheshire). Tough Canadian-bred lilies combine with the equally hardy and fabulously beautiful Connecticut hybrids to form the basis of the Cheshire Bulb Farms' stock.

These lilies really have to be seen for one to appreciate the wide range of colour and beauty they can offer. They come in various shades of lemon, apricot and orange. Some have wide open chalice cups, facing up to the sun, freckled and dusted with purple. Others have turn-back flowers. The blooms are among the biggest I have encountered – gay and beautiful with a glowing warmth in their colours and a silky sheen to their waxen-textured petals. They flower just when the garden needs a fillip – from mid-June until August, when the first flush of roses and herbaceous plants is over and the border is in need of something spectacular enough to focus interest. We like the scent of these hybrids, too. It is fresh and delightful, not at all cloying as is sometimes found in some of the older types of lily.

Their needs are relatively simple – just good border conditions with enough room around them for their foliage to be able to benefit from the light and air. Or you can grow them among low-growing shrubs like the dwarf evergreen azaleas or the small-leaved rhododendrons such as 'Sapphire' or the early species. It helps to dig in plenty of moist peat and coarse sand before planting to ensure the well-drained yet moisture-retentive compost that lilies like, with a lacing of rotted manure or general fertilizer to start them off.

In spring, when their noses begin to push through the earth, the lilies should be given a mulch of rotted bracken, peat or leaf-mould because this type of lily is stem-rooting. They need the soil to be top-dressed as they grow, giving the new roots something to feed on as they extend and, by strengthening them, improving their soil-anchorage.

To their original range of Canadian-bred, Asiatic hybrids, Cheshire

Bulb Farms are adding more and more of the Connecticut hybrids. These lilies are very popular in America where some of the more recent hybrids are costing as much as five dollars a bulb, wholesale. Like the ultra-hardy Canadian strains they are bred from tough Asiatics such as *L. cernum*, *davidii*, *wilmottiae*, 'Maxwell' and *tigrinum*. From these ancestors they have inherited the readiness to increase that makes them such a satisfactory garden buy. Like the Canadian hybrids, too, they are the right height for the average garden – 75–90 cm (2–3 ft) – and they quickly build up into flowering clumps.

Somewhat lily-like in aspect, *Galtonia candicans*, the Cape hyacinth, from South Africa, is beautiful with tall spikes of creamy, hanging bells. The bulbs are usually not too expensive to buy and should be planted in March. They look well growing at the back of herbaceous plants or among low shrubs. To encourage them to become permanent they should have good soil and plenty of light and air.

CHAPTER THIRTEEN

Walls – a climatic bonus

Because of the proximity of the buildings, and the warmth they reflect, town gardens tend to be warmer than their country counterparts. So the tiny town garden with its walled protection often offers a chance to grow plants that would not succeed over much of the country away from the south and west coast. Typical of these are some of the Chilean shrubs, though these must have a moist, peaty soil if they are to succeed. But even this is not too difficult to arrange if they are planted in a raised bed. Tub cultivation would also be suitable, but here one must remember that roots in an above ground pot are more vulnerable to frost than they would be if tucked away safely below the soil surface. It pays, therefore, to use a double pot system, planting the shrubs into tree pots and then placing them in decorative tubs or urns with an insulating layer of straw, bracken or peat between the two containers.

One of the most rewarding of the Chilean shrubs is the lantern bush, *Crinodendron hookeranum* ($2-2\frac{1}{2} \times 1$ m ($6-8 \times 3$ ft)), which makes an upright pillar of evergreen growth. The large lantern-like flowers are produced when the shrub is young, and their scarlet shows up vividly against the dark green lanceolate leaves. In our North Wales garden this species flowers twice a year, in late May or June and again in September. Planted against a white-painted or stone-faced wall, with dianthus and nerines at its feet, its corner will be one of the major attractions of the year. We find that the nerines spear satisfactorily through dianthus foliage and that the blue-green leaf 'mats' offer effective winter protection to the bulbs. Like most Chileans, the lantern bush will flower in sun or semi-shade.

A spectacular companion from the same part of the world is *Desfontainea spinosa*, with holly-like, evergreen leaves which (unlike holly) are borne opposite to each other on the stems, and tubular, trumpet flowers which shade from scarlet into gold. The desfontainea is slightly more fussy about moisture than the crinodendrons and whereas the latter will grow and flower freely even in near drought conditions, the former must have a moist soil, which can most conveniently be provided if a generous quantity of damp peat is dug in at planting time.

Some eucryphia species come from Chile, but the two members of the genera most likely to prove satisfactory in the enclosed conditions of the tiny garden are the hybrid *E.* × *nymansensis* 'Mount Usher', which is evergreen, and the deciduous *E. glutinosa*, which adds the beauty of autumn tints to that of its white rose-of-Sharon flowers. *E.* 'Mount Usher' flowers when very young, but it often bears double blooms mixed with the typical singles of the genus. The eucryphias need similar conditions to the desfontainea. *E.* × *intermedia* 'Rostrevor' is also compact enough for our purpose.

Also worth trying is the Chilean fire bush, *Embothrium coccineum lanceolatum*, in the 'Norquinco Valley' form which is extremely hardy. Making a tall, slender shrub with scarlet, honeysuckle-type flowers that wreathe the branches in late May and into June, the only drawback is that it does not flower for the first few years. So splendid is it, however, that – taking up as little room as it does – it is worth waiting for.

Winter jasmine, *Jasminum nudiflorum*, is a plant that every gardener seems to find space for, somewhere on a wall or even as a cascading, mounded bush, so as to enjoy the joyful beauty of its golden stars through the winter months. On a warm wall in a town garden, however, the larger-flowered and even more beautiful *J. mesnyi* (syn. *J. primulinum*) will often succeed. From March to May this scandent shrub produces its large semi-double flowers. It is unfussy about soil but needs a trellis or mesh panel into which its branches can be tied. Near it might be trained the summer-flowering, fragrant *J. officinale* 'Affine', the white flowers of which are tinged with pink on the outside.

To no other gardener are his surrounding walls more important than to the owner of the backyard or tiny, enclosed garden. Distempered, or painted white or cream so as to reflect the light, and equipped with square mesh trellis or plastic mesh panels, they offer the opportunity almost to double the potential flower-power of the garden by offering a vertical face for display while at the same time taking up very little in the way of width.

Not only can wall shrubs such as the blue ceanothus or yellow-fruited pyracanthas be trained flat against the wall surface, but the trellis or mesh panelling will enable numerous scramblers and climbers to be grown there too. At their base one can site the more tender bulbous subjects such as nerines, the winter-blooming, rhizomatous *Iris unguicularis*, and the beautiful and graceful agapanthus, the blue lily-of-the-Nile, of which the newer Headbourne Hybrids provide a variety of shades on sturdy stems, coupled with a great degree of hardiness.

One rose which, although not a true climber, is best trained against a wall is the single-flowered *Rosa chinensis* 'Mutabilis', the flowers of which pass through shades of crimson, rose, coral, chamois and yellow without any of the vulgarity or muddled ugliness of which 'Masquerade' and some if its successors are guilty. Subtle and lovely, *R. c.* 'Mutabilis' needs a background of natural stone or a white or cream-washed wall to show off its beauty. Against a red brick wall it could only be a disaster.

The ampelopsis, a tendril-climbing vine, has a cultivar of weaker and more restricted growth than the rest, which is ideal for planting in tiny gardens. This is *A. brevipedunculata* 'Elegans', the vine-like leaves of which are densely mottled with white and tinged with pink. Hillier's of Winchester are, as far as I know, the only current source of supply.

In the south, against a sunny wall, *Campsis* 'Madame Galen' can be relied on to flower well. With its larger trumpets of salmon-red it is more worth planting than the vigorous *C. radicans*. *C. grandiflora*, however, might have a place on an arbour, or an out-building, in full sun where its growth can ripen sufficiently to produce its spectacular orange and red trumpets.

Clematis are of course naturals for enclosed gardens. Free-flowering in any aspect (but some retaining their colour best out of full sun), the large-flowered hybrids appreciate their roots being shaded by any lowly plant such as nepeta or the beautiful but tender *Hebe hulkeana*, the rounded leaves and large, lavender-blue flower panicles of which justify its being offered space at the base of a sunny wall.

Nowadays there are many clematis hybrids, but for reliability and general ease of cultivation I think the following are hard to better: 'Nelly Moser' (striped), 'Comtesse de Bouchaud' (rose-pink), 'Hagley Hybrid' (larger-flowered rose), 'Mrs Cholmondely' (lavender-blue), 'The President' (plum-purple) and 'Lasurstern' (deep blue). Of these 'Hagley Hybrid', 'Comtesse de Bouchaud' and 'Mrs Cholmondely' being hybrids of 'Jackmanii' should be pruned hard to within three buds of the old stem in February. All the other hybrids need have only surplus or tangled growth removed after flowering.

Of the ivies, *Hedera colchica* 'Dentata Variegata' is vigorous enough to cover a high wall. Its leaves are bright green shading to grey and margined with creamy yellow. It is hardier than *H. canariensis* 'Variegata' and almost equally effective. Its cultivar, 'Paddy's Pride', is irregularly splashed with deeper yellow in the centre and is invaluable to give a sunny effect. The *H. helix* cultivars such as 'Buttercup', 'Glacier', 'Gold Heart' and 'Silver Queen' are less vigorous and smaller-leaved. They are more suitable to decorate low retaining walls or to carpet the ground in dry areas. The variegations are less distinct when grown in dense shade.

The climbing hydrangea, *H. petiolaris*, is strong-growing and self-clinging and is useful to cover a north-facing or shaded wall. Deciduous, its large flower corymbs are showy, with several large, conspicuous, white, sterile florets surrounding the beady, pale green, fertile flowers. It may need initial support until the aerial roots by which it climbs become fully active.

We have already discussed the honeysuckles in Chapter Eight, so we might now consider the too seldom seen and lovely mutisias, which well merit the sheltered, warm conditions of the tiny enclosed garden. Three species are currently obtainable, *M. decurrens* with brilliant orange large daisy flowers with flat, shining petals, *M. ilicifolia* with lilac-pink daisies, and *M. oligodon* with salmon-pink petals. Of these *M. decurrens* is the most difficult and least hardy. If you can give it a warm, partly shaded west wall and a compost of rich, sandy loam you will have a good chance of success. *M. ilicifolia* and *M. oligodon*, with tiny, prickly holly leaves from which curling tendrils emerge to help them to climb, are much easier. Of these *M. ilicifolia* is the most vigorous but *M. oligodon* will also cover a wall up to $2\frac{1}{2}$ m (8 ft). When grown against a wall all you need is the support of trellis or a plastic mesh panel, but *M. oligodon* would also be happy scrambling over hardy fuchsias, phlomis, hebes or similar lightly built shrubs.

The passion flower, *Passiflora caerulea*, beloved because of its symbolism, is nonetheless a plant of intrinsic merit, beautiful with its white sepals, and corona of conspicuous filaments, which are blue at the tips, white in the middle and purple at the base, and so give the flower the appearance of being colourfully zoned. The passion flower blooms freely from June until frost and is hardy on a warm, sunny wall with good drainage.

Solanum crispum 'Glasnevin' is a scrambling wall shrub which bears masses of purple-blue, gold-centred potato-flowers. It blooms freely all summer and into autumn and will grow well on both chalky and acid soil. It is reasonably hardy on a wall, or against an outhouse.

Most of the true vines have the disadvantage of being rather over-vigorous for tiny gardens. They can be useful, however, if needed to cover an arbour or pergola where it is necessary to give screenage from high-rise buildings. One of the hardiest is *Vitis* 'Brant', which bears bunches of dark grapes which are quite sweet to eat. Its leaves colour attractively to dark red and purple in autumn with conspicuous greeny yellow veins. *V. coignetiae* is extremely vigorous, but it too can be used for screening purposes. It possesses the finest leaves of all. Large and rounded, with a heart-shaped base, they are felted beneath with rust-coloured tomentosum. In autumn they turn to magnificent shades of crimson and scarlet.

In addition to the vines, wisteria, particularly the beautiful white *W. venusta* with its fat ivory racemes and bronzy young leaves, might also be used to drape a strongly made pergola type of arbour.

As stated earlier in the book, one of the simplest and most satisfactory methods of training climbers is to provide panels of plastic mesh, pegged to the wall or fence at each corner. Trellis, too, will provide a decorative solution. Very useful, though, for tying in wall shrubs or roses are the new plant ties (available through iron-mongers) manufactured by Bostik. They consist of a specially toughened pin, with a flat head for hammering, attached to a tie which can be looped over the stem and then press-studded 'home' to the pin. Currently retailing at 22p per pack of ten, including VAT, these are good value at today's prices, providing as they do such a neat and ingenious answer to an old problem.

CHAPTER FOURTEEN

Bedding and annuals

However tiny the garden, the judicious use of bedding plants and even of a few selected annuals, raised *in situ*, helps a great deal to keep it colourful and pretty.

One has to be careful, though, to avoid a spotty effect, and I myself do not like the garishness of an overall bedding scheme. Better far, I think, to use bedding plants cautiously to supplement more permanent plantings. Ideally, bedding subjects should be planted out in window-boxes, troughs and containers, or kept to focal sites near the windows, flanking steps or embellishing a sitting out place. Wallflowers, antirrhinums and dahlias can also be used to fill in gaps in the flower border or to complement shrubs. The place for gladioli, in my opinion, is among herbaceous plants, where they can spear through the foliage, to take over the display from earlier-flowering subjects.

For spring, wallflowers and Brompton stocks are the ideal bedding plants, with forget-me-nots as runners-up. In our own garden, we prefer to use our forget-me-nots under shrubs and in the flower border, instead of in a formal scheme. I always shake them out as I lift them each year so that they may shed their seed and ensure a spreading mist of blue for the following spring.

In many gardens, Brompton and East Lothian stocks will last for several years, building themselves up into objects of considerable beauty. In such places, provided space can be spared, it pays to leave them in the ground, perhaps sowing a ribbon of scarlet flax, or blue and rose viscaria, to provide summer colour.

Most tiny gardens are sheltered enough to give the early strains of wallflower a chance to bloom. The Early Phoenix varieties in various colours, and Thomson and Morgan's 'Harbinger' (reddish brown), 'Golden Mascot' and 'Early Wonder Mixed' are all reliably precocious in a sunny sheltered site.

Winter-flowering pansies are often a success under such conditions, and buying pelleted seeds will give one the chance to sow them where they are to bloom. A mid-spring sowing should give flowers from autumn on, through all but the coldest spells of winter, and during the spring. Winter-flowering pansies are also particularly useful for positions in semi-shade or for north-facing window-boxes or tubs where they will bloom well. Perennial under suitable conditions, they should be allowed to carry on from year to year.

Also useful for shady sites are the showy polyanthus primulas, which are available in shades of blue and pink, as well as brick red, crimson, white and gold. Blackmore and Langdon's strain, Barnhaven Polyanthus, and the Pacific Giants are all good. With polyanthus, again, when obtainable it pays to sow pelleted seed. Then, from a March sowing, the plants may well be in flower the following autumn.

For the tiny garden, the expenditure on pelleted seed is more than justified by results as the pelleting not only makes success more sure but also gives larger plants which come into bloom more quickly. Modern pellets are made up from various growing substances that are sensitive to moisture. Rolled around the seed, the pellets break down rapidly for germination and do not stick to the emerging shoot. They do, however, need to be kept thoroughly moist until germination has taken place. By making it possible to handle tiny seed, their use enables one to place the seed exactly where one wants it. This makes direct outdoor sowing possible, thus enabling the plants to develop deeper, more penetrating roots, to give greater resistance to drought and stronger and more uniform growth.

For summer bedding, the choice is wide. Petunias are among the first favourites as they flower as well in semi-shade as in sun and sometimes have the bonus of scent. Personally, though, I dislike the striped and 'starburst' varieties. I would say, enjoy by all means the doubles, the ruffled singles, and the new pendulous strains which are so useful for hanging baskets and window-boxes, but avoid the garish bicolours which with their restlessness seem the antithesis of the gentle grace and beauty that one associates with the petunia.

For colour, as well as for scent, one should not forget the nicotianas, of which flower arrangers will pick the 'Lime Greens' strain and 'Sensation Mixed', which contain not only a few of the lime-greens but also a green-throated white, dusty purple, velvety maroon and chocolate-pink.

Sweet peas, too, are welcomed for their scent; dwarf varieties of sweet peas such as 'Cupid' and 'Knee-Hi' are the most suitable for the tiny garden. A cool, slightly moist soil suits them best so, in the conditions usually found in the kind of plots with which we are dealing, it would be helpful to dig in a generous quantity of well-soaked peat before sowing or transplanting. This should be supplemented by bone-meal, rotted compost or concentrated manure.

To get the plants off to a good start, it pays to sow them indoors in February in tiny individual pots. John Innes Number 1 suits them well or they can be sown in one of the proprietary peat-based composts, provided they are fed with Liquinure or some similar compound. Once the seedlings are through, start the hardening-off process by leaving the window partly open during the day; or transfer them to a cold frame and raise the light whenever there is no frost. As soon as possible, leave off the glass altogether. Planting-out time varies, as with most other subjects, according to district. In warm places the young plants can go out in early March. Over most of the south they can be set out in mid-March, but in bleak areas, they should wait until the end of the month, or even into April. One has to be guided by the season.

The dwarf sweet peas, whatever the seed catalogues may say, do best with a little support. This may be given by twiggy sticks or one may use strips of plastic mesh. A pretty effect can be obtained by planting in clumps and using cylinders of mesh for support.

In the south, and in sunny gardens, zinnias will succeed, although they seldom do well in the north. Where they get enough sun they are delightful, with their sturdy rosettes in so many lovely shades. The dwarf varieties are particularly useful for tiny gardens.

It is difficult to imagine a summer garden without the antirrhinum, the old-fashioned snapdragon, but there are now so many different varieties that it is difficult to know which to choose. I think that the tall F1 varieties are rather overpowering for the tiny garden, so I would play for safety always and go for the rust-resistant strains of medium height. Penstemons are delightful too, and even more graceful with open-throated pastel bells.

Edging plants like lobelia, ageratum and sweet alyssum are all too often misused in all-over bedding effects, and in too many trite and hackneyed schemes. Lobelia, in particular, is so lovely in its own right that full use should be made of its suitability for making pools and rivers of light and dark blue at the front of the border or among the shrubs. It is effective, too, for carpeting roses. Far from harming the roses, by creating a living cover for the soil, such lowly shallow-rooted plants help to prevent the spread of fungal infections, the spores of which are apt to drop to the ground and over-winter there. Ageratum, too, is useful for the same purpose. Neater than the pansy or viola in such a situation, and less inclined to 'climb' than some of the rock plants, lobelia and ageratum make ideal underplantings. Ageratum also looks well when used beneath fuchsias, being more subtle and so showing up the hanging beauty of their flowers much better than do the semperflorens begonias generally used for this purpose.

Pelargoniums and begonias are so expensive now, and so artificial in effect, that I think their use should be confined to window-boxes and containers. Of the other more expensive 'luxury' bedding subjects, the gazanias, arctotis and gerberas can best be incorporated into sunny borders. Gerberas and arctotis look effective beneath standard roses, where their pretty daisy-like flowers can help to soften a formal scheme, while the silvery foliage of the gazania is so attractive that it might be included in a border of 'silvers'. All these bedding daisies, however, may be less expensively supplanted by a plant or two of the hardier perennial South African *Dimorphotheca barberiae* (pink) and *D. ecklonis* (blue-zoned white). These will over-winter safely in a raised sunny position in many areas.

The annual asters are useful for late summer colour, and for the tiny garden they can be used at the front of the flower border instead of wasting precious space on the similarly coloured Michaelmas daisies which are so soon over. Thomson and Morgan offer two cushion-forming strains of aster that are particularly suitable, 'Pepito Mixed', with large-rayed single flowers, and the double-flowered 'Carpet-Ball'. These include all the purples, amethysts, whites, pinks and crimsons that one associates with the harvest festival beauty of the herbaceous asters.

Many people enjoy the French marigolds, and one should not forget, either for the garden or for cutting, the easily grown 'pot' marigold, the calendula, of which an art shade mixture or the new 'Rays of Sunshine' will give flowers ranging from cream and primrose through apricot to orange. These succeed in even the most difficult conditions, and I think one of the reasons I am so fond of them is that I associate them with one of the gardens of my childhood, in an industrial area of the Potteries, so close under the shadow of a steel works that the 'fall-out' rendered impossible the cultivation of anything other than gooseberries, sempervivums, rhubarb and the orange calendula!

The tiny garden cannot afford room for failures, so one must select for direct sowing only those annuals which are certain to come up. The eschscholzias or Californian poppies are sure-fire for a sunny spot in well-drained soil. Seed is obtainable either of the orange type or of art shades in single and double varieties.

Clarkia is another reliable annual, and while I would not use it for bedding and am chary of so-called annual borders (both on account of their flimsy appearance and because they are so likely to have their effect spoiled if one or more subject fails) I like to find room for it somewhere in the garden.

Candytuft is pretty, compact, and reliable enough to have a place in the bedding scheme. Look for it under its official name of *Iberis* and try the Dwarf Fairy strain with closely petalled flowers in lilac, pink, white, rose, carmine and purple. As with the forget-me-nots, seed shaken out over the border after flowering should result in a pretty variety of plants to come up the following year.

Not everyone has the facilities to raise their own bedding plants, so when buying in plants for summer bedding it is important not to make one's purchases too soon. Penstemons, antirrhinums and stocks will not really be ready to go out until mid-May, while the end of the month is soon enough for petunias and asters. Really tender subjects such as zinnias, nemesia, *Phlox drummondii* and nicotiana should wait until all danger of frost is past, which can mean the second week of June in some cold districts.

It is important only to buy plants that have been properly hardened off. Deep green, thick-textured leaves are a reliable indication of this. Buy only plants that are short-jointed and sturdy with leaves of the right colour. Spindly, yellowy plants will have become crowded in their seed-boxes and not been given adequate space to develop.

With wallflowers and Brompton stocks (both for autumn planting), look for compact, bushy plants. Bushiness is the indication that they have been properly transplanted, as is necessary to induce hardiness and sturdy growth that enable them to stand the winter well. Whenever possible insist on getting the Hanson's 'All-double' strain of Brompton stocks (the same applies to the summer-flowering ten-week stocks). Of this strain, only plants with light green foliage should be bought. A dark green leaf colour indicates single flowers, and such plants should have been discarded in the nursery. If this strain is not available you will, of course, have to take a chance. Even the single-flowered stocks are attractive, but an all-double planting does give a more even appearance.

When buying asters, beware of any that have brown marks near the soil level. This is a sure sign of aster wilt and such plants will usually die before flowering. Nemesias are too often overcrowded in the seed-boxes and offered for sale as poor, spindly plants. Reject these firmly and insist on a sturdy, well-branched selection, otherwise you are sure to be disappointed with their flowering and growth.

Pansies and violas may often be purchased already in flower. This is no drawback as it enables you to choose the varieties that appeal to you most. Such well-grown plants, however, do need special care in planting and should have a little, well-rotted compost and some moist peat mixed with the soil before they are set out. Care must be taken, also, to give water whenever needed, otherwise they may start to flag. Short-jointed, bushy plants are the kind to look for.

When buying polyanthus primulas, look for young plants. Beware of those with small, poor leaves and lack of vigour, indicating that they have been propagated from pieces of old, worn-out crown, instead of being grown freshly from seed. Others may have been lifted from the nursery rows after several years of neglect without division. In such cases, even though you seem to be getting a big clump you will still be the loser. Young, strong plants that have been sown the previous May will give the best results.

Pelargoniums that have been grown in individual containers cost more to buy but these give the best results. Always pick compact, short-jointed plants and reject any that are spindly or have been drawn up. With dahlias and tuberous begonias, too, look for those that have been individually grown. Semperflorens begonias, however, can be satisfactory when seed-box-grown.

CHAPTER FIFTEEN

Window-boxes and containers

To be entirely satisfactory, window-boxes should really be tailor-made to the required measurements of each individual house. If they are to be painted, softwood or deal will be the best wood to choose for their construction. Alternatively, teak or red cedar can be used. They will then only need to be oiled in order to protect their appearance, and can look very handsome. The advantage of painted window-boxes, however, is that their colour can be chosen to complement the colour scheme of the house, and as some backyard gardens are rather dreary in aspect painted boxes can go a long way towards brightening the scene.

For the best effect, the boxes should be 25 cm (10 in) or more wide in order to give room for a double row of staggered plants such as antirrhinums or wallflowers, at the same time leaving room for pansies, lobelia, ageratum, dwarf nasturtiums or crocuses to be used as an edging. The boxes can be either square in section or they can taper towards the wall at the base. The base should, however, be not less than 20 cm (8 in) in width and the boxes should be at least 20 cm (8 in) deep to allow for a 17-cm (7-in) depth of compost.

Upper storey boxes need to be fitted with a gutter to prevent water dropping from them. This can best be done by affixing a length of plastic guttering under the front of the box, which should be sloped slightly forwards to encourage surplus water to drain into the gutter. A thin pipe can then be connected to the gutter to lead the water down to a surface drain. The length of guttering should be painted to match the window-box and the pipe coloured so that it merges with the bricks, roughcast or stonework of the house.

It is important that the boxes are securely fixed into position. If the window frames are wooden, it should be possible to use angle brackets for support, screwing the bracket to the window frame and to the bottom of the box. If the window sill slopes, wedges of wood may be hammered into position beneath the box to keep it level. If the window sill is too narrow to support the box fully, it will be necessary to fix slanting brackets beneath the box to give additional support.

Free-standing containers may be in the form of wooden or cement troughs, tubs, pots, urns or sinks. They should, if possible, be light in weight and easily portable – especially if they are to be used on roof gardens or balconies. They should be attractive, yet not so striking as to detract from the appearance of the plants. At the same time they should complement their surroundings.

For the backyard garden of a country cottage or older house, wooden tubs and half casks would be entirely suitable. If they are not obtainable locally, they can be purchased by post (for addresses of suppliers see pp. 154-6).

The type of lightweight, cement planter that is fairly widely obtainable today would be more in tune with the functional lines of modern buildings. And do not despise the useful large pots of green or white plastic. These are lightweight, durable and offer very acceptable growing conditions. Most plant roots appreciate a plastic pot, so much so that planting in an ornamental container and wanting to obviate frost danger to the roots of a special shrub, I always plant directly into a large plastic tree pot of the type mentioned and then sink this into the container, packing the space around with peat or straw.

Wooden tubs or casks should be charred before planting. This can be done by lighting a fire of shavings inside the cask and allowing it to burn until the wood is charred to 3 mm ($\frac{1}{8}$ in) deep. To put out the fire, simply turn the tub upside down on the ground.

Strawberry barrels and pottery strawberry planters offer attractive homes not only for strawberries (which we will consider in the next chapter) but also for ivy, trailing lobelia, pendulous petunias, ivy-leaved pelargoniums, hyacinths, clumps of crocuses and other delightful plants.

Lime-hating shrubs such as camellias and rhododendrons, hydrangeas which are intended to be kept blue, the pretty kalmia (calico bush) and the decorative Japanese maples may be grown in the Royal Horticultural Society's camellia compost of 7 parts turfy loam, 3 parts granulated sedge peat and 2 parts gritty, lime-free sand (parts by bulk). To each bushel of this compost should be added 42 g ($1\frac{1}{2}$ oz) of hoof and horn and 42 g ($1\frac{1}{2}$ oz) of bonemeal. If this is too difficult to make up, an alternative would be to use Fisons Plantgrow, adding lime-free loam and bracken peat if you are able to bring back an occasional sackful from country foraging expeditions.

Plantgrow may also be used for small shrubs, bedding plants and bulbs which are to be grown in window-boxes and containers. Bedding plants do well also in John Innes potting compost No. 2 or in Levington Compost or Bio-Humus. Whichever of the soil-less composts one uses the plants will benefit from being fed with a liquid fertilizer such as Fisons Liquinure every ten days. This feeding is essential for plants being grown in Levington Compost.

Watering of container-grown plants is, of course, most important, the only exception being in the case of fibrous-rooted subjects such as petunias, French marigolds, zonal and ivy-leaved pelargoniums and *Begonia semperflorens*, which actually benefit from the withholding of water for the first few days after planting, while they are becoming established. The compost, naturally, must be watered well before planting, but for the plants to be a little short of water for a few days afterwards stimulates root-formation and action. Afterwards they should be watered regularly. They must never be allowed actually to flag for want of water.

Before applying a liquid feed, make sure that the compost is moist. Water first, then feed, should be the rule. Nasturtiums and French marigolds make leaf instead of flower if they are fed too well, so they should be given only sparing boosts. If grown in John Innes potting compost No. 2 or 3 they will need no additional nutriment.

Choosing plants for window-boxes and containers is always fun. For the plants to be off the ground and so further from the reach of slugs and snails is almost a guarantee of success. Two troubles, however, sometimes beset the owners of window-boxes and containers: I wouldn't call either cats or birds 'pests', but they can be a nuisance in scratching up the plants. Both can be foiled by spreading a mulching sheet of black polythene over the soil, cutting crosses at each planting site, turning back the polythene from the cuts and inserting the plants through the holes. Plant growth will quickly cover the polythene which in any case, being black, is fairly unnoticeable. Alternatively one can fix plastic mesh over the boxes and plant through the mesh.

It is necessary always to take the colour of the container into account when deciding on the planting. For instance, yellow daffodils, yellow, orange, pink or red tulips and all wallflowers would look well in white or green window-boxes or troughs. For blue-painted containers, however, white daffodils, white or pink tulips and blue grape hyacinths, with trails of 'Silver Queen' ivy at the front of the box, would look much more effective. Pink and white Brompton stocks, too, would look better than wallflowers in a blue painted box, while pink and lavender stocks would make a fine combination in a white-painted window-box.

For containers, the range of planting is wider than for window-boxes. Quite large shrubs such as camellias, Japanese maples and dwarf rhododendrons and azaleas can be made at home in them. Hydrangeas, roses and hypericum might also be used, and one could even plant clematis and other climbers provided the containers were placed close to a wall offering trellis or a plastic mesh panel up which they could be trained. Sweet peas and the alpine clematis, *C. macropetala*, can be planted in free-standing containers if a cylinder of mesh is inserted into the compost and held rigid with sticks.

Fuchsias are excellent for providing summer colour in troughs and tubs, particularly the semi-prostrate 'Rose of Castile' (pink and purple), 'Marinka' (cherry red), 'Margaret' (rose and violet), 'Lena' (cream-pink and mauve), and 'Alice Hofman' (pink and blue). Petunias, too, always look well, as do antirrhinums and tuberous begonias. *Campanula isophylla*, with its trailing stars in white or blue, lobelia, and dwarf French marigolds can all be used as edging. Best of all bedding plants for containers, to my mind, are the ivy-leaved pelargoniums, as their trailing habit enables them to cascade over the edge, while their leaves and short-stemmed flowers are also attractive. Lavender and pink varieties might be combined with white, or with white, crimson and magenta zonals, with excellent effect.

Keen window-box and container gardeners will find further information in my book *Window Box and Container Gardening* which, like this volume, is published by Faber and Faber.

CHAPTER SIXTEEN

Pleasing the palate

It is always satisfying to grow something to eat, so, though available space may be severely restricted, most of us like to grow something for the table, even if it is only a few herbs for flavouring in a window-box, or some strawberry plants in a barrel or tub.

Strawberry barrels are not only useful in providing a medium in which one can grow the most delicious of all dessert fruits, but decorative as well. In fact I think it worthwhile to order two or three, using one for strawberries and the others to house such cascading rock plants as aubrieta, dianthus, campanulas and phloxes, or even as homes for spring bulbs, planting dwarf nasturtium seeds among the bulbs, at the top and in each pocket, so that they make curtains of flowering greenery during the summer.

Plant a barrel with perpetual-fruiting strawberry varieties such as 'Sans Rivale' or 'Gento' and you will be sure of strawberries for the table throughout the summer and much of the autumn as well. In addition to the wooden barrels (for addresses of suppliers see pp. 154-6), plastic and earthenware 'planters' can also be obtained. Or you can make your own, buying a sound barrel, scrubbing it well inside and out if necessary, and charring the inside. The planting holes should be bored with a 2·5-cm (1-in) bit at 45-cm (1½-ft) intervals, spacing them irregularly to give a better effect. Drainage holes should be provided at the base of the barrel. You can then fix castors to the bottom so that it can be moved easily if it is to stand on paving or concrete.

Efficient drainage is essential, so it is important to put a 15-cm (6-in) layer of broken crocks or stones at the bottom of the barrel. A central core of drainage can be provided by putting a piece of piping or a small drainpipe in the middle, filling it with rubble, and gently raising it to allow the rubble to trickle into position as the soil is added. The pipe is then removed, leaving a vertical drainage stratum down the middle of the barrel.

Any good garden soil makes suitable strawberry compost, but to do your strawberries really well it is worth adding some well-moistened peat and 56 g (2 oz) of bonemeal. These should be laced evenly through the mixture. Failing this, use John Innes potting compost No. 3. Plant your strawberries by poking their roots through the holes as the soil reaches that level. Be sure to firm the roots well in before adding more.

A properly made and planted strawberry barrel will go on for years, each season yielding bigger crops. Window-boxes might also be planted with strawberries, and I have even seen them planted in wall pots and hanging baskets with the runners trailing prettily down. The new tower pots are good too. These are interlocking tubes of white plastic. Each section contains two plant pockets and the tower can be built up to a considerable height. Taking up little space being only 23 cm (9 in) in diameter although almost 90 cm (33 in) high, the pots introduce a useful new planting dimension for the small garden.

To ensure success, it is vital to remove the first flush of blossom that occurs after planting, to give the plants a chance to become established and to build themselves up before the strain of fruiting. Watering is important, and an occasional feed of liquid manure will help to ensure full-flavoured, succulent crops.

Runner beans, also, can easily be grown in tubs or half-barrels, the plant being trained up a tripod of poles or a cylinder of plastic mesh. They need plenty of moisture while they are growing, so it will pay to line the base and sides of the tubs with several thicknesses of newspaper soaked well in water. Good garden soil is the best growing medium for them but if this is difficult to obtain John Innes potting compost No. 2 or 3 mixed with moist peat, will be a good substitute. To ensure the peat is well soaked, stab holes in the polythene bag and leave it overnight in a bucket or sink of water. Surplus moisture should then be squeezed out before use.

Runner beans need plenty of food, so they would appreciate well-made compost or bagged manure mixed into the soil before planting. The beans should be set about 30 cm (1 ft) apart and 5 cm (3 in) deep in May. Dwarf beans, too, may be grown in tubs, or in clumps in the flower border. They should be sown in a staggered double row around the edge of the container or in circles in the border. They may also be grown in a trough against a wall with a Netlon panel for support.

Chinese food addicts might like to try Shungiku – the chop-suey green – which can be sown in small patches as required $1 \cdot 2$ cm ($\frac{1}{2}$ in) deep and 10 cm (4 in) apart. As the plants are harvested when they are about 12 cm (5 in) tall they take up very little space in the garden. Cooked like spinach, Shungiku is highly aromatic and can be used to flavour a variety of Chinese dishes.

Bean sprouts, too, have a high nutritional value and are useful in helping the body cells to rejuvenate themselves. Moreover they need no garden space in which to grow. All one has to do is to place the required number in a waterproof container in a warm dark place and keep them watered. Within eighty to ninety hours of sprouting they are ready to eat and are considered to be particularly rich in vitamins of the C and B group.

Salad vegetables are ideal to grow in troughs or tubs. To bring them nearer the light in a shady area they can be grown in raised beds, provided plenty of moist peat is incorporated.

In a reasonably light backyard garden, the problems of how to combine such utility crops with decoratives in a mainly ornamental plan need not be too hard to overcome. I would suggest planting the salading strips as edgings to one or two of the flower beds in the way that the French do in some of their *potager* gardens.

The crimson-lined leaves of beetroot, for instance, are quite ornamental, and it is well worth while sowing a half row in mid-April and a second in mid-May. The seed should be sown thinly and the seedlings thinned to about 30 cm (1 ft) apart. Wet peat should be dug in to conserve moisture, and if sparseness and poverty of soil is a problem, Egyptian Flat-topped Early Beet would give the best results.

Carrots for pulling young and grating might be included in the *potager* beds, half a row being sown in March and the other half in April. 'Early Nantes' is a reliable variety for the purpose.

Chives give a delicate onion flavour to any salad and are in any case attractive edging plants in their own right. They can be grown either from seed sown *in situ* or bought as plants. Yearly division keeps them healthy and helps them to increase at the same time. The leaves should be kept well cut and any flowers removed as soon as they appear.

Garlic, if liked, can be grown – and this effects a considerable economy as it is often expensive to buy. It is best grown from cloves planted 5 cm (2 in) deep and 20 cm (8 in) apart in March. When the leaves die down in August, the bulbs should be lifted, dried in the sun for a few days and then hung in a cool dry, place.

Lettuce, of course, is the main ingredient of most salads, and a constant supply for the summer and autumn is the target at which to aim. To this end, sowing should be made every three weeks from March to July. The purchase of a row of cloches will enable an even longer period of supply to be ensured. Expensive glass cloches are unnecessary and difficult to store. Tunnel cloches of rigid clear plastic will be found quite adequate.

Sow half a row at a time, choosing a variety like 'Trocadero Improved' or 'All the Year Round' for the main summer crops. Both these are the round, cabbage type of lettuce. 'Little Gem' is a small cos variety and is very sweet, with crisp, semi-blanched leaves (Thomson and Morgan offer pelleted seed of this variety). The small, cabbage-type 'Tom Thumb' is also an attractive lettuce for restricted space.

To lengthen the season into the autumn, sow a short row in early August and another at the end of the month. These plants should be thinned to 20 cm (8 in) apart and covered with the cloches at the end of September, or a little earlier if the weather is cold. They will be ready for cutting at the end of November and into December. 'Winter Density' is a good variety for late cutting, while for sowing under cloches in October 'Arctic King' can be relied on to produce salading in March and April and into May.

Mustard and cress can, of course, be grown on flannel or moist peat on an indoor window sill, or you can make sowings directly into the garden or in boxes or tubs outside. Spring onions can be sown in March or April for pulling in June. 'White Lisbon' is the best variety for the purpose.

Parsley is both decorative and useful, for salads, garnishes, and sauces. I find, in spring it germinates best if a kettleful of boiling water is poured down the drill before the seed is sown. A sowing in July will provide parsley through the winter and spring.

Radishes can be sown under cloches from December to April or outdoors in spring. The larger winter radishes are good to grate into a salad. They can be sown from July to August and left in the ground to be pulled when required. 'Black Spanish' or 'China Rose' are varieties to choose, while I find 'Icicle' one of the best of the more usual spring and summer varieties. It is long and white in the root and very crisp and sweet. 'Scarlet Globe' is also good.

People with sunny backyards and patios often like to grow outdoor tomatoes. These have a better chance of ripening well if sited against a sunny whitewashed wall which will reflect the maximum light and heat. Many owners of tiny gardens will have to buy in their tomato plants from a nurseryman or from the local market. In this case it is essential to make sure that the plants have been well hardened off. At the time of planting, they should be about 20 cm (8 in) high, sturdy and with deep green leaves free from any yellowing or striation. Discard any leggy or weak-looking plants. The popular dwarf 'Amateur' is a good variety to choose.

If you have a miniature propagator, of course, you will want to sow your own tomato seed. In this case you cannot choose better than the tall 'Outdoor Girl' or dwarf 'Sleaford Abundance', which is in effect an improved 'Amateur'. Like the older variety it is suitable for raised bed or tub cultivation, growing only to a height of about 45 cm (18 in) and spreading to form a wide mound. Another new and quick-ripening variety is 'Pixie'. The seed should be sown about the end of March in John Innes potting compost No. 1 at a temperature of around 13°C (55°F). As soon as germination is complete, the boxes should be placed in the window of a warm, sunny room and watered carefully so that the soil is never over-wet. As soon as the seedlings are big enough to handle they should be pricked singly into 7·5-cm (3-in) pots. At this stage one of the soil-less composts such as ICI's Kerimure with the corresponding liquid feed is ideal. The plants should be hardened off in a cold frame ready for planting out at the end of May.

An alternative method with 'Amateur' or 'Sleaford Abundance' would be to sow the seed outdoors in a raised bed or in pots in early May, sowing three seeds to a station and covering them with large inverted jam jars. Thin out to one seed per station, and leave the jam jars on as long as possible. This avoids disturbance due to transplanting.

With pot-raised plants it is important to avoid undue disturbance during transplanting to bigger pots or containers. The plants must not be set too deeply, the roots just being covered with about 1 cm ($\frac{1}{2}$ in) of good soil. Stakes should be provided at once and the plants tied loosely to them. Plants set directly into the soil, should have a distance of at least 37 cm (15 in) between them.

Apart from the dwarf varieties, it is important to keep the plants to a single stem in order to get good-sized fruits. This means removing the side shoots as soon as they can be handled. They can then be pinched out between the finger and thumb without leaving a scar. Smokers should note, however, that virus can be transmitted via tobacco to the tomato plants, so they should be sure to use rubber gloves when carrying out this operation.

Tomato plants grow quickly and must be kept tied to their supports with green twine or raffia. Be sure not to tie too tightly as the stem keeps expanding while the plants are in growth. In the first week of August, the plants should be stopped – that is, their growing tips should be cut out. This will direct the energies of the plants into swelling and ripening their fruit. Stopping should be done with a sharp knife, cutting the main stem at one leaf above the last truss of flowers. This will result in the plant sending out more side shoots, and care must be taken to remove them all. It pays, too, to remove all lower leaves as soon as the trusses directly below them have ripened. Any yellow or diseased leaves should also be removed as soon as noticed. Liquid Tomato 'Plus' (ICI) or Bio Tomato Food should be fed regularly every ten days or so to offset deficiencies and to ensure a good crop.

In the tiny garden, pot-grown fruit trees are a good proposition for the garden owner who is keen to produce something to eat. Fruit trees on suitable stocks grow well in pots and can be very decorative as well as useful. The most suitable size pot for young trees is a 30-cm (1-ft) one, but after a few years they should be transferred to 45-cm (18-in) pots, after which they can be expected to go on and fruit for twenty years or more.

It is important to ask for pot-grown bush trees when ordering and ask the nurseryman to supply trees grafted on suitable dwarfing stock. Good varieties of apple for the purpose are Charles Ross, Laxton's Superb and Cox's Orange Pippin, all of which will help to ensure cross-pollination for each other; Williams's Bon Chrétien and Peregrine peach are self-fertile and need no pollinator. It is sometimes possible, also, to buy family apple or pear trees with several compatible varieties grafted on the same tree.

A good compost for potting trees consists of: 3 parts fibrous loam (by bulk), 1 part well-rotted manure, and a handful of bonemeal per pot plus a little ground chalk. All pots should be well soaked before planting. To avoid frost damage, stand the pots inside an outer container for the winter, placing an insulating layer of peat or bracken between the two, cover the surface of the pot also with 5 cm (2 in) dry peat, and then encase the containers in sacking or two or three layers of black polythene, which can be removed when frost danger is past.

Oblique cordon apples are worth planting as a division within the garden. They take up little space and their yield is good. Apples seldom do well espaliered on walls, but such a method is often successful with pears and even for choice plums, and gages such as Jefferson's Gage and Coe's Golden Drop. Most fruit trees are subject to pests and diseases. Aphis may be troublesome and should be sprayed with Hexyl Plus (PBI), when the tree is in bud, as a control. Peaches should be sprayed with Dithane (PBI) in mid-February and again in autumn, to prevent the fungus disease, peach leaf curl. All red or blistered leaves should be burned. Mildew may affect apples and pears, and any infected trees should be sprayed with Mildew Wash (SBK) after cutting off the affected shoots.

A small sunny front garden could be attractively utilised as a herb garden, or one could devote a small section of a backyard to herbs. A paved square with a bush of rosemary in the centre, surrounded by L-shaped beds devoted to marjoram, thyme, sage, borage, the various mints, lemon balm and hyssop, and with a plant or two of the statuesque lovage or angelica for height, could be effective for much of the year. Even in winter, the various types of sage, thyme, rosemary and lavender would provide foliage interest.

Marjoram (*Origanum*) has a pretty golden-leaved form, *O. vulgare* '*Aurea*'. Culinary sage comes in several different forms with coloured foliage ranging from pink and mauve to various shades of green and gold, and there are many varieties of mint of which *Menthum rotundifolium*, the round-leaved apple mint, is best for mint sauce. There is also the refreshing eau-de-cologne mint, *M. requienii*, with purplish leaves, spearmint with neat small foliage, and a form with golden variegations. The roots of all the mints are, however, invasive, so they are safest grown in containers sunk in the ground.

A large size of empty fruit tin would serve the purpose of limiting their wanderings.

Lemon balm is a perennial with grey-green leaves that are pleasantly fragrant to crush. They make a flavoursome addition to thyme and parsley stuffings and offer a contrast in shade to the bright green of the hyssop.

Fennel, like parsley, is not truly hardy in all places and may have to be sown afresh each year. Its large golden flower heads are decorative and may be dried for winter use in the house.

Most of the thymes make low mounded bushes or prostrate mats and are useful to edge the herb beds. With lemon thyme and the various species with woolly or variegated foliage there is plenty to choose from.

Along with these basic culinary herbs, the gay bergamots, the taller sages (including the beautiful *Salvia sclarea turkestanica*), blue borage and pot marigolds can be associated to add further colour and interest.

CHAPTER SEVENTEEN

Rock and water

It is not necessary to have a rock garden in order to grow alpines but many tiny gardens might benefit in appeal from the inclusion of a small rocky outcrop – perhaps in conjunction with a cobbled background. Alternatively, a container might be devoted to the growing of alpines, set among two or three characterful rocks, or a raised bed might be devoted to the billiard table type of small rock garden, the inmates of which would benefit greatly from the sharp drainage inherent in such a situation. Again, one might make an alpine border, with several attractive rocks sunk into position, using a selection of easy, fairly strong-growing rock plants to make a ribbon border beside a path or to edge a bed of larger-growing perennials.

Whatever scheme one decides upon, an important factor in its success will be the provision of a suitable compost. John Innes potting compost No. 2 with some leaf-mould and additional grit and sand suits all alpines except the calcifuges, while a top-dressing of chippings will help to keep away slugs and snails, and, by sharpening the drainage, prevent winter damp from rotting away the crowns of the plants. Lime-sensitive subjects such as the dwarf rhododendrons and azaleas, some of the gentians and lithospermums and the Asiatic primula species could be happily accommodated in a compost based on 2 parts peat, 1 part lime-free loam or leaf-mould and 1 part sand (parts by volume).

The positioning of the rocks is important. For the best effect any rocks used should be set with two-thirds of their bulk buried. It is important, too, to ensure that all the stratum lines run the same way so as to give the effect of a natural outcrop. Further, all the rocks should tilt backwards, thus affording protective drainage to any special plants that might be set up against them. In an acid compost, for instance, the beautiful ramondas and shortias might successfully be grown in such a position.

For a table bed or trough, the alpine year might start with tiny bulbs such as *Iris histrioides*, crimson and white forms of *Cyclamen orbiculatum*, and the sunny yellow *Iris danfordiae* (which has to be replanted each year). Towards spring, would flower hoop petticoat daffodils, scillas, chionodoxas and crocus species, mingled with early saxifrages such as the sulphur *Saxifraga* × *elizabethae*, golden 'Haagii' and pale pink *S. irvingii*. In summer would follow small dianthus such as the rose-pink, clove-scented *D. freynii*, and rose-red *D. neglectus*, along with uninvasive campanulas like the starry violet *C. arvatica* and *C. pulla*, the harebell-like *C. cochlearifolia* and the starry blue *C. garganica*. With them might mingle the little androsaces, *Delphinium nudicaule* in red and chamois, crimson and purple forms of erinus, easy gentians, the apple-blossom *Geranium dalmaticum* and the delicately veined, pink *G. sanguineum lancastriense*, small penstemons such as the lilac-flowered *P. menziesii* and the crimson *P. rupicola* and various thyme species.

In peaty composts in shade, one might accommodate *Meconopsis quintuplinervia* (Farrer's harebell poppy), ramondas, shortias, *Gentiana angulosa* (for spring), *G. farreri* (for summer), *G. macaulayi* and the autumn-blooming *G. sino-ornata*. The deep blue *Cyananthus microphyllus* (syn. *C. integer*) would also be happy, as would haberleas, *Iris cristata* and *I. lacustris*, *Jeffersonia dubia*, lewisias, lithospermums, *Mimulus primuloides* and *M.* 'Whitecroft Scarlet', silenes, and the entrancing soldanellas.

Tougher and more able to take care of themselves are the plants suitable for an alpine border or edging. There one might use the mossy saxifrages, pretty alpine phloxes such as 'Betty', 'Eva' and *douglasii*, *Campanula carpatica*, *Geranium sanguineum*, *Dianthus* × *allwoodii*, bright blue *Ceratostigma plumbaginoides* (the leaves of which crimson most attractively in full sun), the dwarf *Astilbe chinensis pumila* with plumes of lilac pink, the easy *Gentiana lagodechiana*, and *G. septemfida*, small primroses such as *P. altaica* and the *juliae* hybrids, along with small narcissi such as 'Beryl', 'Dove Wings' and 'March Sunshine'. To add colour in winter, the more compact *Erica carnea* heaths such as 'King George' and 'Vivellii' could be planted.

Water associates well with rock, and the tiny garden might include an outcrop of rock and alpines in a pebble bed setting, with a sunken prefabricated pool offset by marginal plantings of *Iris sibirica*, mimulus, Asiatic candelabra primulas and marsh marigolds such as the double 'water goggles' *Caltha palustris* 'Flore-pleno'.

June is the best time to plant a water garden. Before planting, the pool or container should have a 12-cm (5-in) layer of loam, laced with bonemeal, placed at the bottom. This should be allowed to settle and the water then trickled in so as not to churn it up. A 45-cm (18-in) depth of water would suit mini-water lilies such as the waxy white, sweetly scented *Nymphaea odorata minor* or the small pink *N.* 'Laydekeri Lilacea' and the red *N.* 'Laydekeri Purpurata'. All water lilies need soil in which to grow. They can be planted in small plastic pots or fruit punnets, with a piece of turf placed upside down over their roots and bound into position with string.

For the pool to be clean and healthy, one or two oxygenating plants must be included. The water violet, *Hottonia palustris*, the water hawthorn, *Aponogeton distachyus*, or the stock-like *Sagittaria saggitifolia* are all suitable. Fish might also be added. Your local pet shop will advise you about the number and type according to the size of your pool.

Charming water gardens may also be made in tubs, which can either stand independently, perhaps on cobbles or decorative paving, or be sunk into the garden. Any watertight half-cask or tub will do, or you could even use a green plastic plant tub, providing the drainage hole was plugged with watertight mastic. Any barrels or casks should first be properly cleaned and then have their insides charred as described in Chapter Fifteen.

Rocks may be used, set on the 12-cm (5-in) layer of soil at the bottom of the container, to build up pockets at the edge of the tub. In these, soil should be added to provide homes for marginal aquatics, such as *Iris laevigata*, *Myosotis palustris*, the water forget-me-not *Hypericum elodes*, the marsh St John's wort, or the flowering rush, *Butomus umbellatus*, with bronze young leaves and heads of flowers like those of a small, pink agapanthus.

To give a natural effect, it is important to disguise the edges of any tub or pool sunk into the ground. This can be done by setting flattish rocks irregularly round the margins so that they overlap the rim. Semi-aquatic plants such as mimulus, marsh marigolds, *Iris kaempferi* (the Japanese, clematis-flowered iris), rodgersias, astilbes and primulas may then be set irregularly between the rocks to give a natural effect.

Often tubs may leak at first, so it is as well to fill them with water and leave them for a few days before sinking them into the ground. Usually, then, the staves will swell and the tub become watertight.

If leaks persist, a little clay should be worked into a putty-like consistency and rubbed into the joints. Then, provided the tub is kept filled, it will remain leak-proof indefinitely.

Casks sunk into the ground to form a series of little pools can be extremely effective in the small garden, and the surrounding area can be either cobbled or set with rocks and planted with a mixture of alpines and other plants such as the small willow, *Salix boydii*, the Japanese acers, rodgersias, astilbes and bergenias: the aim being to give a furnished and luxuriant effect.

When installing the tubs, holes slightly deeper than the containers themselves should be dug out and soft soil, free of stones, placed in the bottom of the hole and trodden firm. The tubs should then be set in with their rims 2·5 cm (1 in) above ground level. More soil should then be packed around the tubs and tamped down so that the tubs are firmly held. This will help to prevent expanding pressure, when the water is frozen forcing apart the staves and making the tub leak. It will not seriously interfere with the masking of the margins by rocks and plants.

Sometimes a newly planted pool will be cloudy for the first week or two, but this will quickly right itself as the oxygenating plants do their work. Provided the water is kept clear from falling leaves and so long as stale fish food is not allowed to accumulate there should be little real trouble. I would always be wary of magical remedies to clear algae from the water. A better cure is to add extra oxygenators or water snails and fish to make a good natural balance.

CHAPTER EIGHTEEN

Tiny greenhouses and home extensions

So long as one has a sunny, reasonably unshaded part of the garden where it can stand, a little greenhouse can be a good investment, even in the tiniest plot. If you grow your own tomatoes, raise out-of-season salads, force rhubarb and chicory, cultivate early strawberries, sow your own bedding plants, take cuttings of pelargoniums and heliotrope, or over-winter fuchsias and venidiums, the benefits and savings will quickly cover the original cost; or you can settle for a decorative effect with a choice of pot plants and climbers that will thrive in minimal heat.

There are many greenhouse manufacturers, of course, and many models are available nowadays, but for the tiny garden where appearance is as important as results the greenhouse I like best is the 'Circulair' from Humex Ltd of 5 High Road, Byfleet, Surrey. Twelve-sided and of circular appearance, not only is this small greenhouse extremely decorative but, by its construction, it catches all available light. Glassed to the ground also, it offers plenty of growing space. With shelves above the bench, and the ground space also occupied, it has a remarkable capacity for plants, while its all-round ventilator system provides for an intake of air at ground level in addition to the 90-cm (3-ft) diameter dome which can be raised to provide top ventilation.

As an unheated greenhouse, it affords a place to grow and ripen tomatoes, and to raise early salads, fruit and bedding plants. It could also be used as an alpine house, filled with small bulbous plants, rare and difficult primulas, miniature saxifrages, shrublets, and hardy orchids. It is, however, easy to heat, and a small fan heater, such as the Autoheat, even if set low, just to exclude frost, would enable a wide variety of subjects to be grown.

By circulating and warming the air, a fan heater enables satisfactory results to be obtained from a winter temperature as low as $7\,^{\circ}$C ($45\,^{\circ}$F).

A greenhouse so heated can provide winter colour from the scandent ivy-leaved pelargoniums, pot cyclamen, cinerarias and primulas, *Camellia reticulata* and perhaps a scented rhododendron. Pleiones and clivias would extend the bulbous range, while for summer colour one could enjoy all kinds of annuals and lilies in addition to such climbers as the annual ipomoeas, the morning glories, with their velvety, sky-blue flowers; the scarlet *Clianthus puniceus*, the lobster claw; rich purple *Tibouchina urvilliana* (syn. *T. semidecandra*); and the rose-red passion flower, *Passiflora antioquiensis*. A plant of *Nerium oleander*, a sub-tropical hibiscus, and perhaps a bougainvillaea, would help to give the illusion of sunnier climates and make the tiny, cool greenhouse an enchanting place in which to sit on the duller summer days.

Even if there is no place in the garden for a greenhouse, it may be worth considering a sun porch or home extension to give adequate room for sitting in on any chilly but sunny day, as well as offering a home to one or two slightly tender plants such as the scented rhododendrons. A lean-to of this type could provide colour and interest by lengthening the season of pelargoniums and begonias, enabling one to have spring bulbs in early bloom, and giving facilities for raising bedding and pot plants.

Two main features, however, must be given priority if the maximum benefit and pleasure are to be obtained. First, adequate ventilation must be ensured, and, second, large picture windows should be included to frame the garden and trap the sunlight. Ventilation louvre windows create less draught than the large-opening types, while roof insulation will provide extra winter protection and help to cut down the condensation associated with plastic roofs. Even better growing results, however, would follow the choice of a glass roof to give extra light. So one has to decide whether priority should be given to the economy of an insulated roof to cut heating costs or the additional light to benefit plant growth.

From the point of view of appearance, textured wall panels, a base of red cedar or teak, reconstituted stonework, and the use of adhesive tiles in swirling Spanish patterns to clad the rear wall, might be considered. Tiled patterns might add to the visual appearance of the floor also, while a brick-built trough against the rear wall could be provided with trellis panels, enabling perpetual-flowering pelargoniums to be trained into a living curtain. Hanging and wall baskets could be used to give additional colour and interest, while a triangular saucepan rack, painted white, might stand in the corner offering shelving for pot plants but taking up little space. With a paraffin heater or turbo-fan to keep out frost, such a lean-to could provide protection for a fair number of plants as well as enabling one to make the most of the sunshine and obtain an illusion of outdoor living on any suitable days throughout the year.

PART TWO

Garden Designs

I The artist's front garden is a very small town plot on a busy street. She has trained *Chaenomeles japonica* and a 'Mermaid' rose along the back railing in an attempt to prevent paper and other forms of rubbish blowing in.

A central-heating boiler is situated under the path at the left of the garden and heat and fumes from this make it difficult to grow anything at that end. Cytisus and *Vinca major* do well as they will put up with these conditions, and a group of pansies thrives throughout the summer.

Malus floribunda, a prettily-arching pink crab-apple, gives height to the extreme right of the garden, and at its foot in spring it has crocuses, daffodils and scilla. These are followed in summer by the coppery day-lily *Hemerocallis fulva*. There are two shrubs – *Viburnum burkwoodii* for spring blooming, and *Hypericum* 'Hidcote' for summer.

Planted around and between the shrubs, polyanthus, pansies, antirrhinums and geums give colour through spring, summer and into autumn.

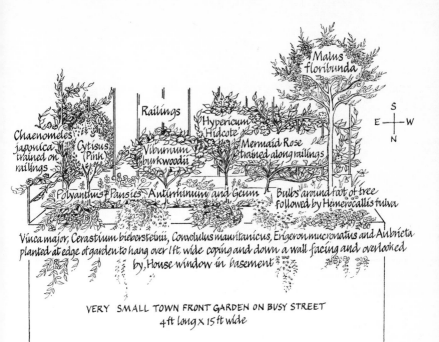

Malus floribunda

Railings

Chaenomeles japonica trained on railings

Cytisus (Pink)

Viburnum burkwoodii

Hypericum Hidcote

Mermaid Rose trained along railings

S / E — W / N

Polyanthus & Pansies   Antirrhinum and Geum   Bulbs around foot of tree followed by Hemerocallis fulva

Vinca major, Cerastium biebersteinii, Convolvulus mauritanicus, Erigeron mucronatus and Aubrieta planted at edge of garden to hang over 1 ft. wide coping and down a wall facing and overlooked by House window in basement

VERY SMALL TOWN FRONT GARDEN ON BUSY STREET
4 ft long x 15 ft wide

A very wide piece of coping at the top of a deep wall into a basement area takes up a quarter of the four feet of the garden. This wall is facing a house window, so to make the view as pleasant as possible, plants that will hang over the coping are put at the edge of the garden. *Vinca major* makes very long trailers which by the end of summer are about twenty feet long. It blooms in winter and early spring, adding its effect to that of aubrietas. In summer *Cerastium biebersteinii* with small, white flowers and silver leaves, makes a pretty contrast with the tender *Convolvulus mauratanicus* with its exquisite lavender-blue flowers, and *Erigeron mucronatus*, a tiny daisy which blooms daily from the end of June until the middle of September.

It is a garden in which the plants have been carefully chosen to solve the particular problems of the site and is successful in providing a long-flowering selection of shrubs, perennials and rock plants that are attractive when viewed from the street or the windows of the house.

2 Unusual paving textures can be useful in offsetting the 'sameness' of a pocket-handkerchief front garden that is similar in size and shape to all the others in the road. In this north-facing example cobbles have been chosen in place of a lawn. Their rounded irregularity contrasts well with the smooth surface of the concrete path.

To emphasize this contrast of texture, concrete planters stand on the cobbles: with their varied plantings they help to add an air of individuality to the plot. Chaenomeles (Cydonia) is an attractive subject to train under the window which faces the road.

Facing north as this garden does, and measuring only twenty feet from the wall of the house to the road, the planting had to be restricted to subjects which do well in shade: this is no drawback as there are so many lovely bulbs and ferns, in addition to herbaceous plants such as foxgloves, primulas and hellebores, which thrive in shady conditions.

Plant shelves in the angle of the house and garden wall can be used

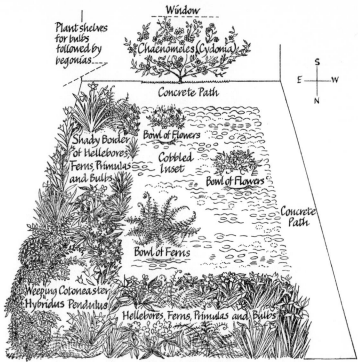

Window

Plant shelves
for bulbs
followed by
begonias

Chaenomeles (Cydonia)

S
E — W
N

Concrete Path

Shady Border
of Hellebores,
Ferns, Primulas
and Bulbs

Bowl of Flowers

Cobbled
Inset

Bowl of Flowers

Concrete
Path

Bowl of Ferns

Weeping Cotoneaster
Hybridus Pendulus

Hellebores, Ferns, Primulas and Bulbs

NORTH FACING FRONT GARDEN
20 ft long x 15 ft wide

to grow more bulbs and ferns, begonias and a wide variety of shade-loving pot plants.

In the corner, nearest the road, the weeping *Cotoneaster* 'Hybridus Pendulus' is grown on a grafted leg to catch the maximum sun. In optimum conditions this cotoneaster can be grown on the flat and allowed to follow its natural habit by creeping over rock-work or covering a surface of paving. Its lovely, bright berries are especially freely borne.

The wide border shown in the plan is intended to help to make the plot look larger, sited as it is to one side. An asymmetric planting of this kind helps to confer an illusion of space.

3 Three different paving textures are used to add interest to this small, square front garden. The path is made of brick, stone flags are used for the area nearest the house, while cobbles provide the setting from which rises a circular raised bed, surrounded by a brick-built low wall and containing an apple tree.

Small spring bulbs, followed by dwarf nasturtiums, surround the tree to make a colourful feature, while two tubs filled with bedding plants stand nearby on the cobbles to provide additional colour.

Spaces have been left in the flags for the planting of assorted heaths of the *Erica carnea* and *vagans* species for winter and summer colour. The well-known *E. vagans* 'Mrs Maxwell' with its bright raspberry-pink, bottle-brush spikes has been chosen for summer, while *E. carnea* 'Springwood' with its white flowers, and the purple-pink *E.c.* 'Winter Beauty' will give colour at the darkest time of the year.

Alpine borders on either side of the path are planted with the easier alpines which can be relied on to give a good show without swamping their neighbours. They include various dianthus hybrids,

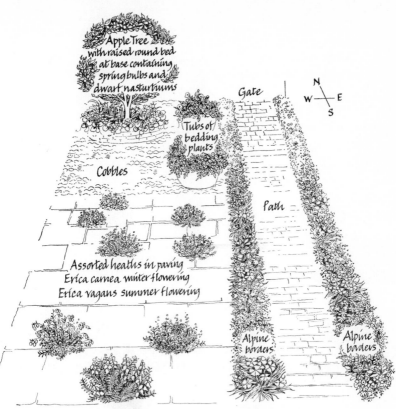

Apple Tree
with raised round bed
at base containing
spring bulbs and
dwarf nasturtiums

Gate

N
W — E
S

Tubs of
bedding
plants

Cobbles

Path

Assorted heaths in paving
Erica carnea winter flowering
Erica vagans summer flowering

Alpine
borders

Alpine
borders

EASY TO MANAGE FRONT GARDEN
20ft long × 20ft wide

helianthemums, sedums, lithospermums, *Campanula carpatica* and *turbinata*, prostrate veronicas, double buff-coloured allyssum and the single lemon form, the pink *Geranium endressii* and white *G. sanguineum* 'Lancastriense', *Polygonum vaccinifolium*, one or two aubrietas (strictly sheared back after flowering), phlox 'Eva' and 'G. F. Wilson', and the sturdier mossy saxifrages. Through and among these spear such small spring bulbs as muscari, species crocus, the true jonquils and *N. bulbocodium*, the gay hoop-petticoat daffodil.

4 Seaside gardens always present a problem, due to the wind and the presence of salt in the air. Grey, sun-loving plants usually do well, as do many of the herbs, so it was decided to use herbs set in beds among cobbles to give an approach to this cottage by the sea.

Boundaries offer an additional planting room in such a restricted space. A hedge of rosemary was chosen to divide the path from the one belonging to the cottage next door. On the right-hand boundary is a close boarded fence, three feet high: this provides shelter and support for the tall-growing fennel and angelica which are as decorative in the garden as they are useful to the cook.

To border the road, an earth-cored wall was constructed of beach stones, cemented together. On top of this a hedge of Hidcote lavender presents a fragrant approach.

A rounded bed of herbs forms the central feature of the garden. Here, various mints, horehound, lemon balm, and golden marjoram surround a bush of *Artemisia abrotanum* (wormwood). Pockets and small beds in the surrounding cobbled paving provide homes for the

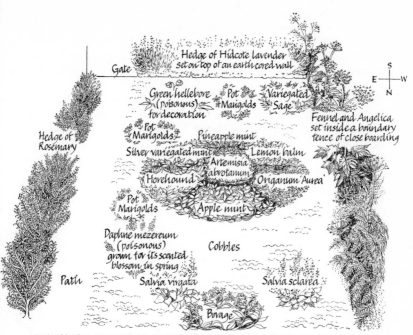

Image labels (top to bottom, left to right):

Gate

Hedge of Hidcote lavender set on top of an earth cored wall

S / E — W / N (compass)

Green hellebore (poisonous) for decoration

Pot Marigolds

Variegated Sage

Fennel and Angelica set inside a boundary fence of close boarding

Pot Marigolds

Pineapple mint

Hedge of Rosemary

Silver variegated mint

Lemon balm

Artemisia abrotanum

Horehound

Origanum 'Aurea'

Pot Marigolds

Apple mint

Daphne mezereum (poisonous) grown for its scented blossom in spring

Cobbles

Path

Salvia virgata

Salvia sclarea

Borage

SUNNY HERB GARDEN AT FRONT OF SEASIDE SEMI DETACHED HOUSE
20 ft long × 20 ft wide

grey-leaved *Salvia sclarea*, bright blue-flowered borage, variegated sage and pot marigolds for colour. Two poisonous but decorative apothecary's plants, the scented *Daphne mezereum* and the green hellebore are also grown. For the nervous, or where there are children, these last two could be replaced by culinary sage and thyme. Thyme, in any case, might replace one of the clumps of marigolds, and would be welcomed by the cook.

5 This was a conventional long, narrow back yard, with all its problems. To save labour and costs, much of the original paving has been left in position. A sitting area nearest the house is divided from the remainder by a brick flower-box, and a circular bed raised above the paving contains scented bedding plants such as wallflowers and heliotrope.

A shrub border containing variegated evergreens and evergrey shrubs is set to one side of the main length of the site to give an impression of width. An oval bed of floribunda roses three-quarters of the way down the yard shortens the distance immediately in view of the house, to create an effect of further space.

A miniature water garden has been created by sinking three half-casks into the paving: they are edged with semi-aquatics and, each cask containing a small water-lily, they add charm to the garden for much of the year.

At the far end of the site, a white-painted trellis against the north-facing wall carries trained cotoneasters to add the brightness of their berries in winter. The winter jasmine at the right-hand corner of the terrace will be trained to interweave among the cotoneasters to provide the cheerful juxtaposition of starry yellow flowers and scarlet berries.

Winter brightness is further taken care of in the shrub border by *Ilex* 'Golden King', by far the best of the variegated hollies, and *Elaeagnus pungens* 'Maculata', with dark green foliage illuminated by splashes of daffodil yellow.

Left of the terrace, *Ceanothus* 'A. T. Johnson' is trained against the wall. This evergreen bears bright blue flowers in two flushes, the first in May, the second in autumn, but can be pruned in spring to concentrate the blooming into one main September burst.

Spring colour will be provided mainly from bulbs, bedding plants, and the alpines that edge the slightly raised bed of floribundas. Here aubrieta and alyssum have been planted for the purpose, interspersed with campanulas and *Stachys lanata* (lamb's ears) to give summer interest. The stachys is useful for cutting.

Sun-loving shrubs in the border against the south-facing wall include *Cistus creticus* for its butterfly flowers, rosemary and santolina (cotton lavender) for their fragrance, and the spectacular *Phlomis fruticosa* (Jerusalem sage) with its golden crozier flowers and grey-green leaves which are valuable for flower arrangement.

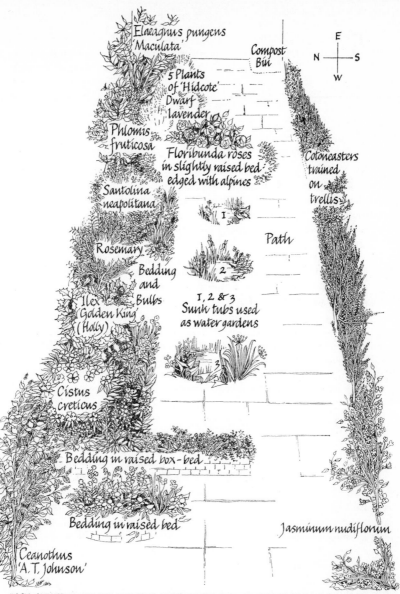

Elaeagnus pungens 'Maculata'

Compost Bin

N E S W

5 Plants of 'Hidcote' Dwarf lavender

Phlomis fruticosa

Floribunda roses in slightly raised bed edged with alpines

Cotoneasters trained on trellis

Santolina neapolitana

1

Path

Rosemary

Bedding and Bulbs

2

Ilex 'Golden King' (Holly)

1, 2 & 3 Sunk tubs used as water gardens

3

Cistus creticus

Bedding in raised box-bed

Bedding in raised bed

Jasminum nudiflorum

Ceanothus 'A. T. Johnson'

EASY MAINTENANCE FOR MAXIMUM EFFECT IS THE KEYNOTE OF THIS BACKYARD CONVERSION

40ft long x 15ft wide

6　The owner of this south-facing garden insisted on year-round interest with the minimum of work, so emphasis was laid on plants with attractive foliage in addition to flowers. Easy-care subjects such as the bergenias and hellebores, scented mahonia and variegated ivy cater for winter interest as well as providing effective ground cover.

Seasonal colour is obtained from a large tub of bedding plants positioned on the paved sitting area near the house. This informal patio will be a sun-trap, facing due south and sheltered as it is from the east by the large outhouse. The winter jasmine will flower well against the south-facing wall and the dwarf lavender used to divide the sun-bathing space from the rest of the garden should yield plenty of fragrance. If something more colourful is wanted, however, the lavender could be replaced by bedding plants.

The constitution of the shrub border can be varied according to taste. If maximum privacy is wanted for the sun-patio as in this case, tall subjects such as forsythia, philadelphus (mock orange) and weigela can be used to obtain quick screenage. If this is not a consideration, the situation offers an ideal opportunity to cultivate such beautiful, though less hardy, shrubs as the scented *Choisya ternata*, *Cistus cyprius* with its purple blotched, snowy saucers, hardy hibiscus, the pineapple-scented *Cytisus battandieri* and similar treasures.

Beyond the shrub planting is a bed of floribunda roses for cutting, backed by the large single-flowered, yellow, climbing rose 'Mermaid', and purple clematis. A clipped hedge of the lime-tolerant, tall *Erica terminalis* (Corsican heath) screens the compost bin.

Camellias at the end of the garden and a trained pear and peach add a touch of luxury without taking up too much space. A small informal lawn provides the necessary, restful touch of green, besides forming a useful contrast in texture with the paving, and offering an alternative place for sitting, should the sun spot near the house become too hot.

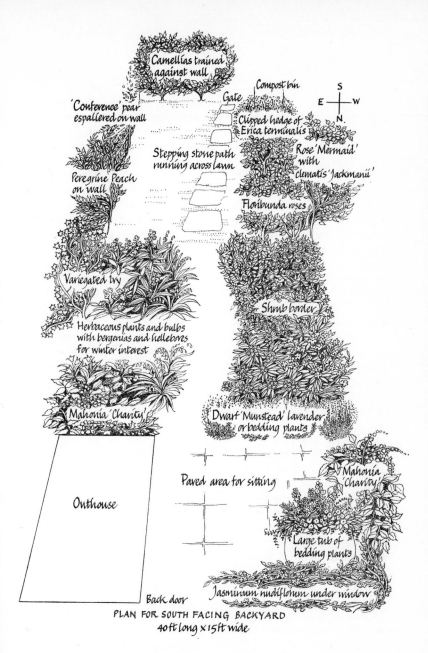

Camellias trained against wall

Compost bin

E · S · W · N

'Conference' pear espaliered on wall

Gate

Clipped hedge of Erica terminalis

Rose 'Mermaid' with clematis 'Jackmanii'

Peregrine Peach on wall

Stepping stone path running across lawn

Floribunda roses

Variegated Ivy

Shrub border

Herbaceous plants and bulbs with bergenias and hellebores for winter interest

Mahonia 'Charity'

Dwarf 'Munstead' lavender or bedding plants

Mahonia 'Charity'

Paved area for sitting

Outhouse

Large tub of bedding plants

Back door

Jasminum nudiflorum under window

PLAN FOR SOUTH FACING BACKYARD
40 ft long × 15 ft wide

7 Some backyards are noticeably dark, causing the plants grown in them to become spindly and drawn. This can best be offset by raising the beds to a height of a foot or more. Material for containing walls need not be expensive as one can use the setts or bricks removed from the yard: in this design the original bricks have been left and those removed from the planting area recycled to raise the beds. Plant shelves in the corner between the wall and the house give sheltered growing space for pot plants and have a pleasing decorative effect when viewed from the arbour which has been placed at the far end of the garden, facing due south to make the most of the sun. Cross-timbers on top facilitate the training of climbers to give this sitting-out place screenage from nearby tall buildings. Stout supports are needed to carry the wisteria. Clematis varieties can be chosen to give a succession of flower. The wall at the rear of the arbour is painted white to reflect the sun.

Pyracantha 'Buttercup' on the west wall, near the gate, is recommended on account of its compact habit, useful in a small space, and its bright yellow berries which are not taken by the birds as are the bright red ones of other species.

City gardens need a refreshing splash of green, especially when so much of the area is paved. The rounded bed of grass is simply for decoration. It is backed by low-growing neat shrubs such as potentilla, caryopteris and cistus, selected to give a succession of interest throughout the spring and summer, with some evergreens among them for winter 'furnishing': this, too, is the function of the variegated ivy trained on the opposite wall.

Alpines need good drainage and sunshine if they are to succeed, and against the rocks of the raised bed against the west-facing wall they should do well. They are balanced by a free standing Japanese maple grown in a tub.

The raised bed for bedding and biennial plants near the house provides a colourful outlook from the window of the main living room and adds height and a focal point of interest when viewed from the arbour.

This garden needs minimum upkeep but is tidy and interesting for much of the year.

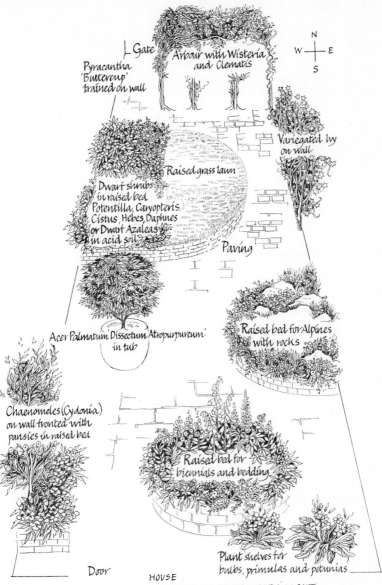

Gate

Arbour with Wisteria and Clematis

Pyracantha 'Buttercup' trained on wall

N
W   E
S

Variegated Ivy on wall

Raised grass lawn

Dwarf shrubs in raised bed Potentilla, Caryopteris, Cistus, Hebes, Daphnes or Dwarf Azaleas in acid soil

Paving

Acer Palmatum Dissectum Atropurpureum in tub

Raised bed for Alpines with rocks

Chaenomeles (Cydonia) on wall fronted with pansies in raised bed

Raised bed for biennials and bedding

Plant shelves for bulbs, primulas and petunias

Door   HOUSE

GARDEN WITH RAISED BEDS TO CATCH EXTRA LIGHT
42 ft long × 15 ft wide

8 Designing this little shrub garden on acid soil gave me particular pleasure as I could include so many favourite plants, though still reserving some room for sitting out.

It was impossible to concentrate on the owner's favourite *Ericaceae* in so small a space without having some gaps in continuity, so provision was made for colour near the house. Two tubs for bedding plants were strategically placed where they would not conflict with the main theme.

To counter the long, narrow look of the garden, the major part of the shrub planting was kept to one side while the path was curved to be in keeping with the informality of the scheme. The path leading to the compost-heap is well-screened by the spreading *Elaeagnus pungens* 'Maculata' which will grow on any soil and which, with its yellow-splashed foliage, is so useful for winter colour. To complement it, another ubiquitous grower, *Senecio laxifolius*, contributes its generous supply of shapely grey leaves. *Prunus* 'Amanogawa' (maypole cherry) is a particular favourite of the owner, although the upright and more unusual *Eucryphia* × *nymansensis* 'Nymansay', evergreen and with strikingly lovely white flowers in late summer, would have been even more appropriate.

Ericas of the *carnea* species in deep pink and white provide winter colour near the house. A narrow band of the long-flowering bright blue *Lithospermum prostratum* is interplanted with *Narcissus triandrus*, a miniature narcissus with turned-back perianth and drooping silvery bells.

A little further back, the broom *Cytisus kewensis* provides a waterfall of sulphur in spring when it is complemented by blue-flowered rhododendron species. The pink evergreen azalea 'Kirin' provides further spring colour. Both this and the small rhododendrons form permanent shapely foliage hummocks, the colour of their tiny leaves ranging from emerald to scarlet throughout the year.

Heaths such as the showy, rosy-spiked *Erica vagans* 'Mrs Maxwell' and golden-foliaged, white-flowered *Calluna* 'Gold Haze' provide summer interest, as do the large-flowered hydrangeas and golden hypericum.

In the narrower border to the left of the garden, a foreground planting of bulbs and day-lilies, the white-flowered evergreen *Azalea* 'Persil', a pink-flowered camellia and a pyracantha on the wall between them provide colour in all seasons.

The planting is graded in height so that all subjects in flower can be seen from the house.

BACKYARD TRANSFORMED ON ACID SOIL
42 ft long × 15 ft wide

9 Shrub addicts remain shrub addicts whatever the size of the garden at their disposal. Here, the obvious disadvantage that gaps must occur in a main planting of shrubs on such a small site has been offset by the provision of a window box, a container and a raised bed in which bedding plants can be grown. These are all sited near the house.

Further colour may be obtained by planting suitable bulbs at the forefront of the shrubs; certain alpines and even suitable dwarf annuals can be used to fill in the spaces between the shrubs until they are fully grown. Creeping campanulas, sedums, *Polygonum vaccini-folium* and helianthemums would be suitable alpines; while lobelia, run in drifts, or the yellow-and-white limnanthes are two annual subjects that would not be out of place.

Most heaths are calcifuge, growing only in acid or neutral soil, but the winter-blooming *Erica carnea* varieties are a fortunate exception in that they give one the chance to enjoy bright colour during the dark months, even on chalky soil.

In this alkaline garden it would be impossible to include dwarf azaleas, rhododendrons or camellias without the trouble of cultivating them in tubs of lime-free soil, so it was decided to concentrate instead on some of the lovely shrubs which actually do better on lime. Among them are the misty-blue caryopteris and the flame-coloured potentilla which flower in summer, the scented mock-orange, the white flowered, small *Hebe pagei*, the deciduous ceanothus, with its powder-blue plumes, and the upright-growing *Prunus* 'Amanogawa' (apple blossom cherry). *Berberis thunbergii atropurpurea* was added for the long-lasting attraction of its glowing foliage which contrasts well with that of the evergreen, variegated elaeagnus behind it.

The hydrangea may show yellowing of the leaves and suffer from stunting in growth if the soil is very limy. This can be corrected by Murphy Sequestred Iron applied as directed on the packet.

Stepping stones sunk to the level of the lawn offer no obstacle to mowing but prevent wear on the grass. Informally shaped lawns such as this help to create an illusion of space as they curve out of sight.

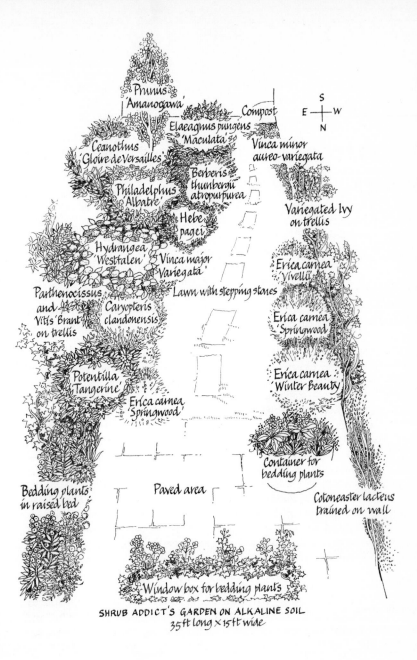

Prunus 'Amanogawa'

Compost

Elaeagnus pungens 'Maculata'

E ┼ W

S / N

Ceanothus 'Gloire de Versailles'

Vinca minor aureo-variegata

Berberis thunbergii atropurpurea

Philadelphus 'Albatre'

Variegated Ivy on trellis

Hebe pagei

Hydrangea 'Westtalen'

Vinca major 'Variegata'

Erica carnea 'Vivellii'

Parthenocissus and Vitis 'Brant' on trellis

Lawn with stepping stones

Caryopteris clandonensis

Erica carnea 'Springwood'

Potentilla 'Tangerine'

Erica carnea 'Winter Beauty'

Erica carnea 'Springwood'

Container for bedding plants

Bedding plants in raised bed

Paved area

Cotoneaster lacteus trained on wall

Window box for bedding plants

SHRUB ADDICT'S GARDEN ON ALKALINE SOIL
35 ft long × 15 ft wide

IO In line with the perennial need to cut the cost of living by growing some of our food, this backyard conversion was planned to give the owner the satisfaction of enjoying freshly picked vegetables, salads and fruit straight from the garden. At the same time it fulfils the twin necessities of providing an attractive outlook from the house and a paved area for sitting in the sun.

A feature is made of the large window box or trough near the kitchen, filled with herbs of the cook's own choice. The strawberry barrel is decorative and yields unsplashed good quality fruit. It may be planted with either the conventional large-berried strawberries or with the so-called 'perpetuals' to give an extended crop.

Colour and flowers for cutting come from the large raised space for bedding plants and from the succession of pansies and bulbs grown in front of the espaliered fruit trees to the left of the path.

A 'hedge' of floribunda roses screens the vegetable plot from the house, and the vegetable garden itself can be made colourful and attractive if thoughtfully laid out. For a limited space such as this, it is best to choose small compact-growing varieties of vegetables – dwarf peas such as Kelvedon Wonder and Little Marvel; broad beans, The Midget; dwarf French beans, Romulus; Brussels sprouts, Early Dwarf; are all suitable. Beet, ferny-leafed carrots, neat shallots and tight round lettuces such as Tom Thumb, can all be used to add eye-appeal. A long row of runner beans could be grown against the east-facing wall – any surplus beans can be frozen or salted for later use.

The family apple tree featured at the end of the garden is delightful in both blossom and fruit. A tree of this kind is ideal for a small space as, having different but compatible varieties grafted on to a single stem, it takes care of its own cross-pollination and yields a succession of fruit. I have suggested marigolds to follow the bulbs in the nearby container as they have a proved deterrent effect upon aphis and various other pests.

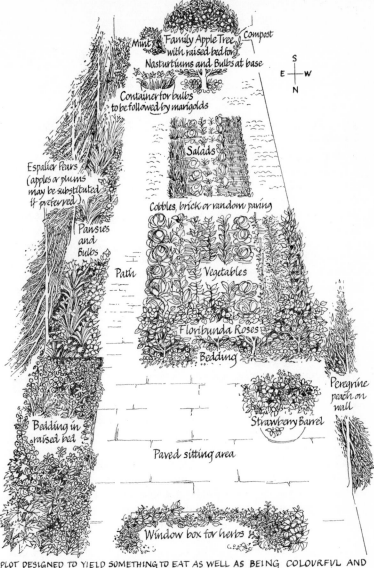

Mint
Family Apple Tree
with raised bed for
Nasturtiums and Bulbs at base

Compost

S
E — W
N

Container for bulbs
to be followed by marigolds

Salads

Espalier Pears
(apples or plums
may be substituted
if preferred)

Cobbles, brick or random paving

Pansies
and
Bulbs

Path

Vegetables

Floribunda Roses

Bedding

Peregrine
peach on
wall

Bedding in
raised bed

Strawberry Barrel

Paved sitting area

Window box for herbs

PLOT DESIGNED TO YIELD SOMETHING TO EAT AS WELL AS BEING COLOURFUL AND
ATTRACTIVE AT MOST SEASONS
42 ft long x 15 ft wide

II Although this is designed to be a flower arranger's garden, it needs to be interesting and colourful when viewed from the house throughout the year.

Long-catkined *Garrya elliptica*, winter jasmine, and the beautiful pink-flowered *Camellia* 'Donation', with variegated ivy grown on a trellis, are chosen for winter, while *Chaenomeles* (the popular 'Japonica') carries the interest into spring. The apple-green *Helleborus lividus* 'Corsicus', spring bulbs and bedding polyanthus pick up the theme, followed by scented white jasmine and floribunda roses in shades of gold and yellow for summer display.

The flower arranger's special interest is catered for by the inclusion of the *Clematis tangutica* with its decorative small yellow lantern flowers, such subjects as fennel, angelica and larkspur, all useful freshly cut or dried, and various foliage materials, for example, senecio, santolina and the purple-leaved *Vitis* 'Brandt' vine.

The island-bed near the house contains a mixture of foliage plants such as the variegated dwarf periwinkle and grey *Stachys lanata*, with pinks, plumed astilbes, graceful dierama (wand flower), tall foxgloves and larkspur, which are useful to lend height to summer arrangements. Plants should be varied to suit personal tastes.

An area of seventeen feet of the garden furthest from the house has been raised to catch maximum sunlight to help the variegated ivy and purple-foliaged vine to colour well, and to aid the flowering of the roses and rock plants. The slightly tender rosemary, senecio, santolina and passiflora (passion flower) will benefit also, particularly in cold districts. The arbour has been designed with overhead supports on which the climbers may be trained to screen the sitting area from the windows of a nearby high-rise block of flats.

NOTE: This plan is really two in one, for the raised part of the garden could easily be adapted to make a tiny and trouble-free garden on its own, replacing the rosemary and senecio with some suitable subjects for cutting suggested in the main part of the plan.

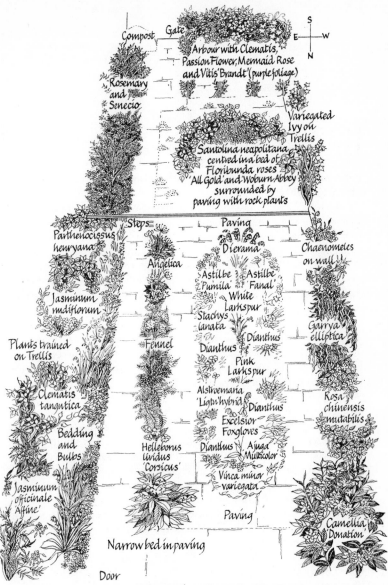

Compost   Gate

E   S · W   N

Arbour with Clematis,
Passion Flower, Mermaid Rose
and Vitis 'Brandt' (purple foliage)

Rosemary
and
Senecio

Variegated
Ivy on
Trellis

Santolina neapolitana
centred in a bed of
Floribunda roses
'All Gold' and 'Woburn Abbey'
surrounded by
paving with rock plants

Steps   Paving

Parthenocissus
henryana

Dierama

Chaenomeles
on wall

Angelica

Astilbe
'Pumila'   Astilbe
'Fanal'
White
Larkspur

Jasminum
nudiflorum

Stachys
lanata
Dianthus

Garrya
elliptica

Plants trained
on Trellis

Fennel

Dianthus

Pink
Larkspur

Clematis
tangutica

Alstroemeria
'Ligtu hybrid'
Dianthus

Rosa
chinensis
mutabilis

Bedding
and
Bulbs

Excelsior
Foxgloves

Jasminum
officinale
'Affine'

Helleborus
lividus
'Corsicus'

Dianthus   Ajuga
Multicolor

Vinca minor
variegata

Paving

Camellia
Donation

Narrow bed in paving

Door

FLOWER ARRANGER'S GARDEN ON TWO LEVELS
42 ft long × 15 ft wide

12 This garden had two main problems – the presence of an ugly wall at its foot and of a large house extension which occupies much of the space. Both have been turned into assets by using them to support climbers.

'Mermaid' and 'Climbing Iceberg' roses were chosen to cover the wall at the end of the garden because they both bloom fairly continually throughout the summer. Interplanted are the 'orange-peel' clematis, *C. orientalis* and the large, white-flowered *C.* 'Marie Boisselot'. Such a profusion of white and yellow-coloured flowers against the high wall does much to lighten the rather restricted area. The use of yellow and white flowers has, in itself, the effect of creating an illusion of space.

On the house extension have been planted the purple *Clematis jackmanii* and the white, scented *Jasminum officinale* which flowers in spring, summer and autumn. It is hoped that in time these will become intertwined so that the walls are covered with flowers for the greater part of the year.

A horseshoe planting of perennials, grouped round the main paved area, forms the basis of the garden. The plants have been selected to give as long a season of interest as possible and are supplemented with a few patches of selected annuals for extra colour. Tall white campanulas, the pale lemon *Achillea* 'Moonshine', columbines, scarlet penstemon, delphiniums, lupins, Siberian irises, astilbes, Japanese anemones and foxgloves combine with ferns and the red Christmas-flowering *Helleborus atrorubens* to give an intriguing display. At the forefront of the border, such low-growing subjects as dwarf stocks, dianthus, polyanthus and *Campanula carpatica* spill onto the paving where a tub of bedding plants provides additional colour.

Herbs for the kitchen have not been forgotten and are grown in a raised bed not far from the kitchen door. Behind them is the striking blue and white *Passiflora caerulea* (passion flower) and next to it a bay tree in a tub gives a traditional touch.

Roses Mermaid and Climbing Iceberg
Clematis orientalis and 'Marie Boisselot'
planted alternately to cover ugly wall

N E S W

Delphiniums, Lupins, Iris sibirica

Penstemon hartwegii 'Firebird'

Astilbe simplicifolia

Mixed plants around foreground of border
Stocks, Pansies, Dianthus,
Polyanthus and Campanula carpatica

Aquilegia vulgaris

Aquilegia vulgaris

Anemone impehensis

Achillea 'Moonshine'

Tub of Bedding Plants

Digitalis purpurea

Paving

Ferns

Campanula latiloba 'Alba'

Helleborus atrorubens

Window

Jasminum officinale to train over window

Clematis 'Jackmanii' to train over windows

Passiflora caerulea planted at back of a box for herbs raised 2ft

Window

House Extension
15ft long x 9ft wide

Door

Clematis montana to train over door

Bay tree in Tub

SMALL TOWN GARDEN WITH LARGE HOUSE EXTENSION
30 ft long x 15 ft wide

A cautionary note on weedkillers and pesticides

Apart from the use of hormone products to over-stimulate and so cause death to broad-leaved plants in lawns, I do not think there is any need for weedkillers in the tiny garden. I am particularly nervous about the use of any products containing paraquat since there have been several tragic accidents following carelessness in its use.

It should not be beyond the ability of most of us to dig out and burn all perennial weeds from our very small plots. Annual weeds are easily dealt with by use of the hand fork or hoe. This should always be carried out before the weeds have a chance to seed. As a further precaution against weed spread, I always consign the uprooted weeds to the dustbin or incinerator, as even well-made compost sometimes fails to kill them all.

Moss on paths has sometimes to be dealt with by the application of an appropriate product, and the cracks between paving can sometimes be host to annoying weed invasion. Where digging out the weeds with an old table knife is likely to prove too back-breaking, the safest method of treatment is by sodium chlorate. Even here a fire risk exists, but ICI have now produced New Sodium Chlorate, which contains a fire depressant. Care must be taken to see that the liquid does not run or seep onto flower beds or neighbouring borders as it will kill any plants with which it comes into contact. If it is used on weed-infested ground, at least six months must elapse before any attempt is made to grow anything there.

The Ministry of Agriculture have recently investigated and approved for amateur use those pesticides which are safe, provided the instructions are observed, and which are effective against the pests listed on the labels. Some of these are as follows:

Derris
Boots Derris Spray
pbi Liquid Derris
Boots Derris Dust

Murphy Derris Dust

Malathion
Boots Greenfly Killer

Malathion cont'd
Murphy Liquid Malathion
pbi Malathion Greenfly Killer
Murphy Malathion Dust
Fisons New Kil Aerosol
Fisons Super Kil

Nicotine
Campbell's Nico Soap
XL All Insecticide (Synchemicals
  Ltd)

Trichlorphon: pbi Kilsect

BHC
Murphy Lindex Garden Spray
Abol-X
Boots Ant Destroyer
ICI Rootfly and Wireworm Dust
Murphy Gamma BHC Dust
Fumite Lindane Smoke Pellets
  for Greenhouses
Fisons New Kil
Fisons Super Kil

Dimethoate
Boots Systemic Greenfly Killer
Murphy Systemic Insecticide
Fisons Super Kil

Formothion
Topgard Systemic Liquid pbi
Toprose Systemic Spray pbi

Tar Oil
Mortegg Winter Wash (Murphy)

Lime Sulphur
Murphy Lime Sulphur

Metaldehyde
Boots Slug Destroyer Pellets
ICI Slug Pellets
Murphy Slugit Pellets

Mercuric Chloride
Boots Calomel Dust
pbi Calomel Dust.

Fungal disorders such as mildew, rust and blackspot attack roses, and mildew and rust also attack various other plants in the garden. Forget-me-nots and Michaelmas daisies are particularly subject to mildew, while antirrhinums and hollyhocks are just two of the other subjects which can be attacked by rust. Benlate (benomyl) systemic fungicide is the remedy I find most effective against all fungus troubles, including some of those which can be troublesome on lawns. Like all the other preparations mentioned in this chapter it should be used with care.

It is important to choose a still day when using either sprays or aerosols and to stand upwind so as not to breathe the mist or get any of the preparations on the skin. All watering cans should be well washed after use. If possible I think it is wisest to keep a special can for hormone weedkiller and to ensure that it is never used for anything else, as it can be heartbreaking to lose treasured plants that may succumb to the merest trace of the preparation.

Garden and nursery suppliers

Bagged Manure
Clavering Compost Ltd, Angmering, Sussex.

Barrels, Tubs, Strawberry Planters, etc.
Barrel House, Chapel Porth, St Agnes, Cornwall.
Garden Features, Millwall Station, Coleford, Glos.

Bulbs
Barr House, Bishop's Hall, Taunton, Somerset (miniature bulbs).
Dobies Seeds Ltd, Llangollen, Denbighs. LL20 8 5D.
Lowland Bulbs, Spalding, Lincs.

Camellias
Hillier and Sons, Winchester, Hants.

Carnations and Pinks
Allwood Bros, Hassocks, Sussex.

Chrysanthemums and Fuchsias
Allan J. Wells, Sugar Stubbs Lane, Banks, Southport, Lancs.

Clematis
Fisk's Nursery, Welteston, Saxmundham, Suffolk.
Pennell and Sons Ltd, 312 High Street, Lincoln.

Compost Bins
Compo-Quick, Deerhurst, Walton, Glos.

Rotocrop Ltd, 848 Brighton Road, Purley, Surrey.

Fibre Glass Containers (antique reproductions)
Verine Products, Folly Faunts House, Goldhanger, Maldon, Essex.

Fibre Glass Pools
Leisure Laminates, Rawreth Industrial Estate, Rayleigh, Essex.

Garden Centre
William Wood and Sons Ltd, Bath Road (A4), Taplow, Maidenhead, Berks.

Greenhouses, etc.
Humex Ltd, 5 High Road, Byfleet, Surrey.
Park Lines and Co., 501 Green Lanes, London N13 4BS (lean-to greenhouse).
F. Pratten and Co. Ltd, Norton Hill, Midsomer Norton, nr. Bath.

Hardy Heaths
Maxwell and Beale Ltd, Corfe Mullen, Wimborne, Dorset.

Hardy Plants
Sunningdale Nurseries, Windlesham, Surrey.

Herbs
E. and A. Evetts, Ashfields Herb

Nurseries, Hinstock, Market Drayton, Salop.

Levington Compost and Peat
Fisons Ltd, Agrochemical Division, Harston, Cambridge.

Paving, etc.
Cotswall, C. I. Black, E. H. Bradley Building Products Ltd, Okus, Swindon, Wilts, SN14 JJ.

Plant Centre
Bodnant Gardens, Tal-y-Cafn, Denbighs.

Plant Supports, Nest Boxes, etc.
Scottish War Blinded, Room B, Linburn, Wilkiston, By Kirknewton, Midlothian.

Pots and Tubs
Patio Design, 4 Ladbroke Grove, Holland Park Avenue, London W.11.

Propagators
Autogrow Ltd, Quay Road, Blyth, Northumberland.
Humex Ltd, 5 High Road, Byfleet, Surrey.

Rock Plants
W. E. Th Ingwersen Ltd, Gravetye, East Grinstead, Sussex.

Roses
David Austin Ltd, Albrighton, Wolverhampton.

C. Gregory and Sons Ltd, The Rose Garden, Chilwell, Nottingham.

Seedsmen
Samuel Dobie and Son Ltd, 11 Grosvenor Street, Chester.
Fogwills Ltd, Friary Street, Guildford, Surrey.
Sutton and Sons Ltd, The Royal Seed Establishment, Reading, Berks.
Thomson and Morgan Ltd, London Road, Ipswich, Suffolk.

Shade Plants
Newlake Gardens, Copthorne, Crawley, Surrey.

Soil-testing Kit
Sudbury Technical Products Ltd, 58 Charlton Road, London, SE3 8TT.

Tower Pots and Strawberries
Ken Muir, Honeypot Farm, Wesley Heath, Clacton-on-Sea, Essex CO16 BJ.

Trees and Shrubs
Hillier and Sons Ltd, Winchester, Hants.
Sunningdale Nurseries, Windlesham, Surrey.
Bodnant Gardens, Tal-y-Cafn, Denbighs.

Water Lilies and Aquatics
Perry's Hardy Plant Farm, Enfield, Middlesex.

Index

Numbers in bold type refer to the garden designs in Part Two.